# 50 Minutes to Better Software Demos

*Apply your sales skills with confidence*

**Matt Gambino**



Viva Books
New Delhi | Mumbai | Chennai | Kolkata
Bengaluru | Hyderabad | Kochi | Guwahati

**First Indian Edition 2011**

**VIVA BOOKS PRIVATE LIMITED**

- 4737/23 Ansari Road, Daryaganj, New Delhi 110 002
  E-mail: vivadelhi@vivagroupindia.net, Tel. 42242200
- 76, Service Industries, Shirvane, Sector 1, Nerul, Navi Mumbai 400 706
  E-mail: vivamumbai@vivagroupindia.net, Tel. 27721273, 27721274
- Jamals Fazal Chambers, 26 Greams Road, Chennai 600 006
  E-mail: vivachennai@vivagroupindia.net, Tel. 28290304, 28294241
- B-103, Jindal Towers, 21/1A/3 Darga Road, Kolkata 700 017
  E-mail: vivakolkata@vivagroupindia.net, Tel. 22836381, 22816713
- 7, Sovereign Park Apartments, 56-58, K. R. Road, Basavanagudi, Bengaluru 560 004
  E-mail: vivabangalore@vivagroupindia.net, Tel. 26607409, 26607410
- 101-102 Mughal Marc Aptt., 3-4-637 to 641, Narayanguda, Hyderabad 500 029
  E-mail: vivahyderabad@vivagroupindia.net, Tel. 27564481, 27564482
- First Floor, Beevi Towers, SRM Road, Kaloor, Kochi 682 018, Kerala
  E-mail: vivakochi@vivagroupindia.net, Tel: 0484-2403055, 2403056
- 232, GNB Road, Beside UCO Bank, Silpukhuri, Guwahati 781 003
  E-mail: vivaguwahati@vivagroupindia.net, Tel: 0361-2666386

***www.vivagroupindia.com***

*Published by arrangement with*

Axzo Press, LLC
562, Willow Brook Office Park
Fairport, New York 14450



ISBN : 978-81-309-1817-4

Published by Vinod Vasishtha for Viva Books Private Limited, 4737/23, Ansari Road, Daryaganj, New Delhi - 110 002. Printed and bound by Raj Press, R-3, Inderpuri, New Delhi - 110 012.

# Table of Contents

# About the Author

Matt Gambino is an expert in the area of demonstrating technology, and he has been helping non-technical salespeople deliver exceptional software demos for more than 15 years. A member in good standing of the National Speakers Association (NSA), Matt has given speeches and led training workshops across North and South America, Europe, and Asia.

Matt has a strong sales, marketing, and product development background, particularly in the area of educational technology. In the course of his work for one of the world's largest educational publishing organizations, Matt has provided thousands of software demos to buyers, clients, colleagues, and vendors.

In addition to coaching salespeople, Matt is an adjunct instructor of computer literacy at Bunker Hill Community College in Charlestown, Massachusetts.

# Preface

An increasing number of "non-software" companies today implement a general strategy to improve profit margins and increase market share: develop new online solutions and services to supplement their traditional product portfolios. Yet the vast majority of sales reps at these firms are painfully uncomfortable with the idea of demonstrating their digital products for an audience. Even seasoned salespeople with years of presentation experience often freeze up when faced with the prospect of giving a software demo.

To help address this "demophobia," non-software organizations spend enormous amounts of time and resources to get their sales reps up to speed on presenting and selling software. One recent study determined that companies spend an average of $2,000 per rep every year just on software product training. Sales reps are often required to endure hours upon hours of hands-on technology instruction; they must peck away at their digital products in order to become "certified users," and they are subsequently forced to rehearse, recite, and repeat exhaustively long product-demo scripts on command.

If this training strategy does not bear fruit (and often it does not), sales management may decide that the majority of the reps are simply not teachable. More money is then invested to recruit, hire, and train product specialists, who are responsible for traveling with the reps and handling the "tech demo portion" of each sales presentation. These folks often carry massive expense budgets because they constantly shuttle back and forth across the country, supporting reps. Because of their endless and chaotic travel schedules, it is often impossible for them to become familiar with any one customer's unique needs—many specialists have to swoop in and get their background information during the walk from the parking lot with the rep. Then it's on to the next city!

As if the increase in sales staff were not costly enough, the marketing department is often put under additional pressure as well—to create expensive, media-rich Flash demos designed to play automatically and augment the rep's live presentation. The self-propelling Flash movie might look and sound impressive (that is, if you overlook the awkwardness of the rep pressing "Play" and standing aside to let the infomercial take over), but each customer typically has distinct requirements that aren't addressed by a generic demo.

It doesn't have to be this way. *Any* sales rep—regardless of his or her technical knowledge—can learn how to deliver custom-made software demos that engage, inform, and most important, *inspire* prospective customers to buy.

This book is written for sales representatives who want to earn more credibility and increase their bottom line by demonstrating software products on their own. A common misconception is that the successful demonstrator of software products must be a computer guru or gadget geek at heart. Not so. In fact, I believe that the non-technical salesperson has the advantage here, simply because the non-techie is often more capable of simplifying the software product and understanding how regular end-users would view it. Put another way, the non-techie might have an easier time describing his product to a cousin at a family gathering. For example:

**Non-techie:** "I sell software that helps attorneys research contract law. Would you mind passing the ketchup?"

**Technical guru:** "I sell software that utilizes an industrial-strength, proprietary database to search for and return new contract statutes based on simple and complex queries, which sit behind a streamlined, Windows-based user interface. When you wake up, would you mind passing the ketchup?"

At the heart of it, the characteristics that make a great salesperson are the same qualities that make a great software demonstrator: a passion for sales, the ability to ask questions and to listen, and a sincere desire to help customers solve problems. This book shows you how to wrap these skills around your laptop so you can show and sell your software in a way that is smooth, simple, entertaining, and easy to understand.

## *Learning Objectives*

Complete this book, and you'll know how to:

1) Outline a customized software demo
2) Prepare and organize your computer to guard against distractions and mistakes
3) Deliver your demo and field questions with confidence
4) Navigate the computer and present like a pro
5) Give effective remote demos by using popular Web conferencing software

## *Workplace and Management Competencies mapping*

For over 30 years, business and industry has utilized competency models to select employees. The trend to use competency-based approaches in education and training, assessment, and development of workers has experienced a more recent emergence within the Employment and Training Administration (ETA), a division of the United States Department of Labor.

The ETA's General Competency Model Framework spans a wide array of competencies from the more basic competencies, such as reading and writing, to more advanced occupation-specific competencies. The Crisp Series finds its home in what the ETA refers to as the Workplace Competencies and the Management Competencies.

*50 Minutes to Better Software Demos* covers information vital to mastering the following competencies:

**Workplace Competencies:**

- Planning & Organizing
- Working with Tools & Technology

**Management Competencies:**

- Informing

# About the Viva-Crisp 50-Minute Series

The Viva-Crisp 50-Minute Series was designed to cover critical business and professional development topics in the shortest possible time. Our easy-to-read, easy-to-understand format can be used for self-study or for classroom training. With a wealth of hands-on exercises, the 50-Minute books keep you engaged and help you retain critical skills.

## *What You Need to Know*

We designed the Viva-Crisp 50-Minute Series to be as self-explanatory as possible. But there are a few things you should know before you begin the book.

### Exercises

Exercises look like this:

**EXERCISE TITLE**

Questions and other information would be here.

Keep a pencil handy. Any time you see an exercise, you should try to complete it. If the exercise has specific answers, an answer key will be provided in the appendix. (Some exercises ask you to think about your own opinions or situation; these types of exercises will not have answer keys.)

### Forms

A heading like this means that the rest of the page is a form:

FORMHEAD

Forms are meant to be reusable. You might want to make a photocopy of a form before you fill it out, so that you can use it again later.

# A Note to Instructors

We've tried to make the Viva-Crisp 50-Minute Series books as useful as possible as classroom training manuals. Here are some of the features we provide for instructors:

- PowerPoint presentations
- Answer keys
- Assessments
- Customization

### PowerPoint Presentations

You can download a PowerPoint presentation for this book from our Web site at www.CrispSeries.com.

### Answer keys

If an exercise has specific answers, an answer key will be provided in the appendix. (Some exercises ask you to think about your own opinions or situation; these types of exercises will not have answer keys.)

### Assessments

For each 50-Minute Series book, we have developed a 35- to 50-item assessment. The assessment for this book is available at www.CrispSeries.com. *Assessments should not be used in any employee-selection process.*

# *P A R T* 1

# Preparing for Your Demo

*By failing to prepare, you are preparing to fail.*"

**–Benjamin Franklin**

## *In this part:*

- The Secret to a Great Demo
- Outlining Your Demo
- Your Best Friend: The IT Administrator

# The Secret to a Great Demo

Before we discuss the magic formula for building a successful software demo, let's quickly look at some of the reasons that demos fail:

- A memorized, boilerplate demo is not customized to meet different buyers' needs.
- The equipment malfunctions (the computer crashes, the Internet connection is lost, the software has bugs, and so on).
- The demonstrator attempts to wing it by substituting glossy presentation technique over command of the material (style over substance).
- The demonstrator focuses on product components that are impressive to him or her but not necessarily to the buyer.
- The demonstrator makes the product look more complex and difficult to use than it actually is.
- Thc demonstrator focuses on software features, not benefits.

The fact is, many demos fail because they are overly complex, difficult to follow, and bloated with features that are irrelevant to the audience. In a word, they are boring.

## *A Two-Part Formula*

So what's the secret sauce for a delivering a powerful demo that makes people eager to buy and use your software product? To find the answer, just watch a rerun of *The French Chef.*

*The French Chef*, starring Julia Child, was one of the first cooking shows on television. Each half-hour episode incorporated the same two-part formula:

- **Part 1:** In the first couple of minutes of the program, Julia would place a magnificent, fully prepared and cooked dish, such as Beef Wellington, in front of the camera.
- **Part 2:** She'd use the balance of the program to demonstrate how to prepare the Beef Wellington recipe from start to finish. And that was that!

Pretty simple, yes? Exactly. That's what made the show so successful. How effective would it have been if Julia Child had tried to *describe* the dish she was going to create at the beginning, and then just started mixing ingredients together? The viewer would not see the benefit until the end of the show (if he or she stuck around to watch). Perhaps the big payoff—the Beef Wellington—would not live up to the hype, based on her description. Viewers would be pretty disappointed, right?

Julia Child understood that if viewers could see how delicious the meal looked in the beginning, they'd stick around to learn how to prepare it. And I promise you—your software demonstrations will earn higher praise and more sales if you take this same approach.

### Show the *End Result* First

When you demo your product, show customers what the software can produce. Then they'll be so interested in the *End Result* that they'll want to learn all about your software.

- **Part 1:** Show the *End Result*.
- **Part 2:** Show how you got that great *End Result*.

## LIST YOUR *END RESULTS*

Many software products can produce *End Results*—such as reports, calculations, or reformatted output—that benefit users. Taking no more than five minutes, list as many of your software's *End Results* as you can think of.

# Outlining Your Demo

You may be saying to yourself: "OK, I get it. But my software includes tons of features and capabilities. What's the 'Beef Wellington' feature of my product? What do I show?" Before we answer that question, let's first consider how traditional demos are usually formulated.

## *The Demo Script Problem*

Many software companies whip up generic demo scripts for new products, and expect sales reps to follow them in their presentations.

### Demo Script

*A document that outlines which features of a particular product should be shown in a sales call or presentation. Some demo scripts are similar to screenplays in that they include speaking lines for the salesperson to recite as he demonstrates a particular feature.*

Product teams and developers love creating demo scripts because they can headline the cool new features *they* worked so hard to build. But keep in mind that the things that may impress a technical developer could very well be meaningless to an end-user. Just because a programmer had to jump through technical hoops of fire to figure out how to program a particularly challenging product feature, it doesn't mean that the *customer* is going to care about that feature.

Demo scripts are also welcomed by the sales reps because reps are usually taught that the script is the blueprint for a successful demo—each step is right there in black and white. All they need to do is memorize the script, perfect their presentation style, and deliver the demo. Buyers will then line up with purchase orders in hand, right? Well, not exactly.

Nothing's that easy. There is no one-size-fits-all solution. If you rely on a canned demo script as some sort of magic potion, you might develop your demo into a polished performance, but you'll find that you miss the sale in many instances because you didn't address the customer's primary need.

### The Solution is Customization

You must customize each and every demo around the customer's need, and shine a spotlight on the *End Result* that solves her problem.

There is some good news here. Because many of your customers are likely to encounter similar problems and have similar needs, you can use the company's basic demo script as a foundation for each of your customized demos.

The trick is to identify common problems in the market, match them with product capabilities, and develop *End Results* that visually represent compelling solutions.

## *Turning an Ordinary Demo Script into a Great One*

Let's say that your marketing or product team has provided you with a generic demo script for a new software product. In this example, you'll be demonstrating a new patient-billing software product designed for medical claims managers.

Here's how to make it better:

1. **List the two or three most compelling product capabilities from the demo script.** If these are not obvious, get some help from the marketing manager or product manager.

   In our example, a compelling capability might be a feature that electronically submits patient claim forms to medical insurance companies via a secure Internet connection.

2. **Identify a primary customer problem that you believe each top capability will solve.** A capability that does not solve a problem is simply a *feature*. A capability that *does* solve a problem can be demonstrated as a *benefit* to the customer.

   In our example, a common customer problem might be sluggish monthly cash flow due to delays in processing insurance claims, or claims being rejected because handwritten forms often contain errors. A tool that automatically creates and submits patient claim forms online would certainly address this problem and *benefit* the customer.

3. **Imagine that you are going to interview a customer about these problems.** Make a list of questions that would get him to admit that he encounters one or more of these problems in his workflow. Try to avoid asking questions that would invoke simple "Yes" or "No" answers.

   For example, if you ask, "Are your claim forms ever delayed in processing?" you're risking a flat "No" response. Instead you might ask, "Could you tell me why claim forms might sometimes be delayed?" The customer can respond in only one of two ways to this question: he can either deny that he's had the problem ("our claims are never delayed"), or he can admit the problem by explaining why the insurance claim forms are sometimes held up in processing.

Here's what your demo chart might look like so far:

| Key Capabilities | Related Customer Problem | Customer Questions to Expose Problem |
|---|---|---|
| Tool that submits claims electronically | Long reimbursement cycles due to delays and rejections in insurance claim processing | Why might the processing of insurance forms be delayed in your office?<br>How is your monthly cash flow affected by these delays? |
| Alert for duplicate patient records | Patient address redundancy results in higher costs for processing return-to-sender mail and loss of time. | How much time is usually spent merging patient records to keep your database clean?<br>How do you handle conflicting addresses during the merge process? |

## DESIGN YOUR OWN DEMO CHART

In the table below, write the Key Capabilities, Related Customer Problems, and Customer Questions to Expose Problems for your software product:

| Key Capabilities | Related Customer Problems | Customer Questions to Expose Problems |
|---|---|---|
| 1. | | |
| 2. | | |
| 3. | | |
| 4. | | |
| 5. | | |

## Creating *End Results*

As you become more familiar with your product and more sensitive to common problems in the market, you will get better and better at aligning product capabilities with customer problems. Here's how:

1. **Collect compelling product capabilities.** Log into the software and closely review each main feature of it.

2. **Identify customer problems that can be solved.** Keep only the features that appear to represent solutions.

   Features that do not solve problems are "nice-to-have," rather than "need-to-have," items. You can keep them on a separate list to refer to from time to time as you visit with customers.

3. **List questions that uncover problems,** and conduct three separate one-on-one customer interviews. In each interview, ask the questions with the intent of getting the customer to identify her primary problems.

   You should see patterns in interview responses. Customers will most likely talk about more serious problems in greater detail. Flag the most severe problems—these corresponding *End Results* will probably be the most compelling during product demos.

4. **Create *End Results*** that visually represent the solutions to the corresponding problems.

   In our example, the *End Result* you would create is a claim report for the insurance company. The completed form might appear on a screen with a Submit Online button, indicating that the form could immediately be sent online to the insurance processing department.

   Building an authentic-looking *End Result* correctly might take some time. For example, to generate a realistic claim report, you might have to log in under multiple sample user profiles, and perform various actions with each profile. This process is a bit tedious, but the payoff is that your customer will more easily visualize how that claim report will look under normal use. (You'll also become a power user that much faster, due to the sheer repetition of the exercise.)

5. **Validate *End Results* with customers**. Pay close attention to how customers respond. *End Results* that invoke the most questions are your winners. Some customers will even get visibly excited ("Yes! That's exactly what I need!").

These *End Results* are the basis for your new and improved demo script. And the new demo script is a foundation on which you can easily build customized demos that align with each of your customer's needs.

***Helpful Tip!*** ***Capture a screen shot of each action you take under one of your sample user accounts. SnagIt (www.techsmith.com) is an excellent and affordable screen-capture tool. Save each screen with a file name that begins with a sequential number, store these files in a folder, and save that folder on your hard drive and on a portable flash drive. You've just created a screen tour that could be used for your own home-grown marketing materials, unexpected situations when an Internet connection is unavailable and you need to show screens offline, and visual examples that help answer customer questions or provide additional information.***

## *How to Outline a Custom Demo*

Don't be put off by the thought of customizing a demo for each sales call or presentation. The time you invested in creating a foundation demo script full of winning *End Results* will enable you to customize your demos faster than you think.

Outlining a custom demo really just entails some of the same steps you took to improve your basic demo script. And the good news is that you've already done the hard part by discovering common problems in the market and creating a portfolio of *End Results* that represent solutions to those problems. Now, you need to:

1. **Determine whether there should be a demo in the first place.** Does the customer (or group of customers) have problems that can be solved by capabilities your software provides? Start by simply asking the high-gain questions you formulated in the process of improving your foundation demo script. Would you agree that the chances are high that your prospect suffers from one or more of the problems you have already listed? If you and the prospect determine that there are problems the software could solve, then a demo is relevant. If there are no problems that your software can cure, move on!

2. **Rank and list the prospect's problems by severity.** List the most painful problem first, and the least painful one last. This could get tricky if the prospect is actually a group of decision makers, but do your best. Place the appropriate product capability next to each problem on the list.

3. **Move the most severe problem to the bottom of the list.** This will be the last problem and capability-solution you present in your demo, and the last *End Result* that will appear on screen. You want it to burn an image into your customers' minds as you close the presentation.

4. **Create a summary and an introduction for your demo.** Writing the introduction as the final step is so much easier, simply because your mind has just engaged in the process of thinking about all the problems your software can solve. In other words, you now know what you're going to show, so your introduction should be a high-level overview of the problems and solutions you are going to discuss.

## WRITE A SUMMARY AND INTRODUCTION

Write a brief summary for your demo in the space below. Use the market's primary problems and your product's capability-solutions as a guide.

Write a brief introduction for your demo, again using primary problems and capability-solutions to guide you.

## *The Importance of Customer Needs*

As a salesperson, you must determine your customers' needs. If your prospect has a need that your product can remedy, you must focus on the primary software features that resolve that particular problem. Think of the customer need as a problem. Determine whether your product can help solve the problem. Then think about the one or more particular capabilities (the *End Results!*) that represent the solution—those are the features to show in your demo. The rest is just noise.

### The Bottom Line

Many demos are simply mindless run-throughs of the product's features. You could probably train a chimpanzee to deliver these demos. They may look polished, but they don't take the customer's needs into account and therefore are of no use. If the customer does not have a problem that your software can solve, don't waste time on a demo! Save everyone's time and move on to the next prospect.

# Your Best Friend: The IT Administrator

Reaching out to the person who manages the presentation room (often there is an IT administrator on staff) is one of the most important parts of the planning process. This becomes obvious when you consider just a few of the many technical problems that could occur on presentation day:

- Presentation room locked
- No projection device and/or projection screen
- Room not wired for Internet access
- Secure network key for Internet connection unavailable
- No power supply (or extension cord to reach it)
- No administrative rights to install software

### YOUR OWN EXPERIENCE

Personalize the list above by jotting down other technical problems that you've run into:

## *Planning Ahead*

The list goes on and on. It's a horrible feeling to do all the customer research, planning, and rehearsing only to run into a technical difficulty that forces the group to huddle around your laptop. Believe me, I know from experience.

You can save yourself from potential disaster by requesting that the IT administrator complete a Support and Equipment form. The IT person is often the last person to know when a vendor has been invited to present (and is none too happy about it!). Many times, she's not even told that someone will be using the technical equipment until the eleventh hour. By sending the form, you are doing the courtesy of giving her a heads-up well in advance of the meeting, so she can plan to be available and help you with the room logistics.

A sample form is on the next page

## COMPUTER SUPPORT AND EQUIPMENT INFORMATION FORM

I am looking forward to our upcoming meeting! To ensure I am prepared to deliver a product demonstration that exceeds your expectations, I ask that you please forward this Computer Support and Equipment Information Form to your IT Administrator. It should be completed and returned to me no later than October 1, 2012. Should you have any questions, please feel free to contact me at 800-555-5555 or anyemail@companyname.com.

| Presentation Information | | |
|---|---|---|
| Date: October 15, 2012 | Start Time: 11:00 am ET | End Time: 12:00 pm ET |
| Location: 123 Main St., Anytown, NY 12345, Center Bldg, Room 567 | | |
| **IMPORTANT! Room should be available at least 30 minutes prior to start time for setup if possible.** | | |

| Support Information | | | |
|---|---|---|---|
| Lab Administrator Name: ______ | | | |
| Email: ______ | | Phone: ______ | |
| Will Lab Administrator be on site to assist with setup? | YES ☐ | NO ☐ | *(If "NO," please ensure that he/she will be reachable at the phone number above.)* |

| Equipment Information | | | | |
|---|---|---|---|---|
| May we use our own laptop and connect to your network for Internet access? | YES ☐ | NO ☐ | *If "YES," please indicate network key information.* | Enter network key:<br>*or*<br>Network key will be supplied on site. ☐<br>Network key not necessary to connect to Internet. ☐ |
| | | | *(If "NO," please ensure lab computer meets minimum system requirements (see attached), and ensure Lab Administrator will assist with software installation/uninstallation.)* | |

Please indicate whether the following equipment will be available:

| | YES | NO | | YES | NO | | YES | NO | | YES | NO |
|---|---|---|---|---|---|---|---|---|---|---|---|
| Projector | ☐ | ☐ | Projection Screen | ☐ | ☐ | Table or Podium | ☐ | ☐ | Audio equipment (microphone, speakers, etc.) | ☐ | ☐ |
| Whiteboard | ☐ | ☐ | Flipchart | ☐ | ☐ | Power supply | ☐ | ☐ | Extension cord | ☐ | ☐ |

| Additional Information |
|---|
| Is there any other information that would help me exceed your expectations? If so, please describe: |

**Please email or fax completed form no later than October 1, 2012 to:**

**S. Anyrep**
**anyemail@companyname.com**
**800-555-5556 (fax)**

**A computer support and equipment information form**

# Part Summary

In this part, you learned how to:

- Make your demos more powerful by showing *End Results* first, and then showing how *End Results* are achieved.
- Create a winning demo script by matching compelling product capabilities with customer problems and creating *End Results* that represent solutions to those problems.
- Outline a custom demo by determining customer needs, ranking problems and End Result solutions, and creating a summary and introduction.
- Avoid technical mishaps by building a relationship with the IT administrator.

*P A R T* **2**

# Preparing Your Computer

***"Organizing is what you do before you do something, so that when you do it, it is not all mixed up."***

**–A.A. Milne (creator of Winnie the Pooh)**

## *In this part:*

- ▶ The Advantages of Technical Preparation
- ▶ The Windows Operating System
- ▶ Web Browsers
- ▶ Other Tools

# The Advantages of Technical Preparation

In this part, you will learn how to organize your computer in ways that will enable you to deliver exceptional software demos. Careful, systematic preparation of your computer before your presentation gives you two distinct advantages: greater audience control, and fewer mechanical errors.

If you've ever visited Disney World and ridden a hosted attraction (such as a cruise through the jungle or a tour of movie history), chances are, you remember the animation around you more vividly than you recall the host who led the tour. This is intentional. Disney makes sure your attention is focused on the theme of the ride itself—the robotic characters, the scenery, the music, and so forth—and not on the person narrating to you.

Company employees (Disney refers to them as "cast members") are trained—rigorously and thoroughly—to be *consistent*. Consistency ensures that the cast member on your vehicle knows exactly where each prop is and where other elements are at all times. Armed with this knowledge, your host can operate so smoothly, so automatically, that her own actions take a back seat to the animation around her. Disney cast members even use numbers, signals, and other codes to react and communicate with one another during unplanned events, so your attention doesn't waiver from the "magic" of the attraction itself.

You will learn to take this same approach when driving your presentations. The goal is to have your decks so clean, so orderly, so *consistent* that you can act—and react—smoothly and without fits and starts. You might think that organizing icons, folders, and files is trivial. But have you ever attended a demo and sat through an awkward silence while the presenter searched for a misplaced file, waited for a stubborn Web page to load, or got an error message because he mistyped a password? Of course you have. Maybe this has happened during one of your own demonstrations. This part of the book shows you how to prepare the computer to guard against hiccups, errors, and mishaps.

There's also an intangible benefit associated with diligent preparation. Going through each step of the process puts you in your presentation mindset and gives you a heightened sense of confidence about your demonstration. Whatever happens, you will know that you're as prepared as you can be technically and that your equipment is set up for you to "walk and talk." It's actually quite comforting.

***Note About Computers:*** ***Because most software demos normally use a laptop and a projector, all references to computers in this part are assumed to be laptops, as opposed to desktop PCs.***

# The Windows Operating System

Knowing how to dress appropriately for a presentation doesn't require you to have a degree in fashion design. Likewise, you don't need to be a computer expert to make simple adjustments to the Windows operating system when preparing for a technical demonstration.

***Note:*** ***Microsoft Vista is used for examples and instructions in this part. If you use another operating system, look at its help system to search for the specific steps necessary to make the recommended changes.***

## *The Windows Desktop*

Let's start with the computer desktop. Turn on your PC and take a moment to look at your own.

- Have you customized your background to display a photo of your children, your spouse, or a recent vacation to the Caribbean?
- Are there icons of document and spreadsheet files scattered about?
- Do you have shortcuts to iTunes, Yahoo! Messenger, and other frequently used applications on your desktop?

### ANALYZE YOUR DESKTOP

Look at your computer's desktop, and imagine that it's projected in front of a roomful of people. Now, put yourself in the position of the audience viewing this desktop for the first time. List the elements you find distracting:

| | |
|---|---|
| 1. ______________________ | 6. ______________________ |
| 2. ______________________ | 7. ______________________ |
| 3. ______________________ | 8. ______________________ |
| 4. ______________________ | 9. ______________________ |
| 5. ______________________ | 10. ______________________ |

## Audience Control

Remember our first objective: *audience control*. You want to make sure that you have your audience's complete attention and that the attendees are solely focused on your message. When your PC is first projected onto the screen, what will your audience think if the first thing they see is a photograph of your dog or your beach vacation? What will they think about their presenter if his desktop is littered with files dropped haphazardly all over the screen?

First, regardless of what audience members think of dogs or tropical getaways, the point is that you don't want them *focused* on those things, not even for an instant. By putting a photograph from your personal life on display, you're immediately giving each member of the audience the opportunity to let his or her mind wander and make all sorts of judgments about you. And maybe they would rather be sitting on a beach than attending your presentation. Why invoke an image of the ocean?

Second, you certainly don't want to give people the impression that you're unorganized. If your screen is a mess of files and other icons, you're reminding people that you have other things to do besides present to them. You're also suggesting that you're scattered, that you don't "have it together."

Study both figures on the next page. Which desktop looks more neat, orderly, and businesslike to you?

**Which desktop looks more organized and businesslike?**

If you were to project the bottom desktop onto a screen, what would the audience members think about when they looked at the projection? Hopefully, nothing! At most, maybe a few people would think that you were neat and orderly. Perhaps *boring*, neat, and orderly. This is fine—as long as you don't trigger them to daydream about something unrelated to your message.

## Clear the Decks

Take the time to clear the decks on your desktop. Get rid of the personal photographs. Move files into folders in your My Documents folder. Throw away unwanted material for good.

If you really want to get organized, consider reading *The Personal Efficiency Program*, by Kerry Gleeson. It's an excellent reference for file organization.

## Use the Single-Click Option

Once your desktop is clutter-free, try enabling the single-click option. This feature allows you to open windows on your desktop by clicking once instead of twice—just like clicking a link on a Web page. It's a very simple change that will help with our second objective: *fewer mechanical errors*. One click is harder to mess up than two. The adjustment is so simple you might think it borders on the ridiculous. But if this setting increases the odds of making your demo look flawless, why not use it?

Here's how to do it in Windows Vista:

1. Click the Start button and choose Control Panel. When the Control Panel appears, it displays either the Control Panel Home page or Classic View. These steps assume that Control Panel Home is displayed.
2. Click Appearance and Personalization to display the Control Panel items in this category.
3. Click Folder Options to open the Folder Options dialog box.
4. Set the desired options by selecting "Single-click to open an item" and "Underline icon titles consistent with my browser."
5. Click OK to close the Folder Options dialog box.

Simple adjustments can make all the difference in the world. In his book *Busting Vegas* (2006, Harper Perennial Publishers), author Ben Mezrick tells the fascinating, true story of a team of MIT students who come up with various methods to increase their chances of winning at the game of blackjack. Some of the techniques the team used were surprisingly uncomplicated and involved precise actions like cutting the deck in a particular location, and so forth. Making such straightforward adjustments before the game began would increase the likelihood of the player "busting" the dealer—and cleaning up with big winnings. As in Mezrick's book, we want the chances of success in our favor—even if some of our fine-tuning increases the odds by one-half of one percent.

## Taskbar

*A bar, usually located at the base of the desktop, used to open and monitor Windows applications.*

For many users, the taskbar is used for little else than getting to the Windows Start menu. Some folks like this bar hidden from the screen until they "pop it up" by pointing to the base of the desktop. But you will do more with this tool.

First, you should disable the auto-hide feature and set the option that keeps the taskbar on top of other windows. Applying these settings allows you to use the taskbar whenever you need it, as well as to avoid the distraction of the bar popping up and down when you move the pointer to the bottom of the screen.

Next, enable the Quick Launch toolbar on the taskbar. By default you should see at least three icons just to the right of the Start button: the Show Desktop icon, the Internet Explorer icon, and the Windows Media Player icon. Delete the Windows Media Player icon (right-click it and choose Delete). Keep the Show Desktop and Internet Explorer icons.

### Preparing the Taskbar

To prepare the taskbar in Windows Vista:

1. Right-click the Start button and choose Properties to open the Taskbar and Start Menu Properties dialog box.
2. Click the Taskbar tab to activate the tab and view the options.
3. Set the desired options by un-checking "Auto-hide the taskbar," checking "Keep the taskbar on top of other windows," and checking "Show Quick Launch."
4. Click OK to close the Taskbar and Start Menu Properties dialog box.

**The Quick Launch toolbar with minimal icons**

### Taskbar Benefits

Why is setting up the Quick Launch toolbar important? Not only does it allow you to start applications fast, but it also enables you to clear your entire screen with a single click of the mouse. For example, imagine that during your presentation, you are juggling four windows: your company's software application, a PowerPoint slide show, and two Web pages. Suddenly, for whatever reason, you must immediately minimize everything on screen. Rather than take the time to hit the Minimize button in each of the four windows one by one (and perhaps accidentally shut down an application), it's faster and safer to click the Show Desktop icon on the Quick Launch toolbar. All windows are instantly minimized, with each application safely running in the background.

## *The Start Menu*

The next operating system element to address is the Start menu. Do the following:

- **Use the Small Icons option when displaying programs.** When you click the Start button, you want the icons that are displayed to use a minimal amount of space.
- **Limit the number of program shortcuts on the Start menu.** You can then display the Start menu during a presentation without showing the audience a bunch of your frequently used personal applications (again, iTunes and the like). In fact, consider clearing this list completely.
- **Empty the list of My Recent Documents** so that you don't show a list of personal documents. Can you imagine accidentally displaying a file name like "Company ABC Confidential Pricing and Sales Strategy.doc" when presenting a product to the Executive Board of Company ABC? That's a situation we all want to avoid.

### Preparing the Start Menu

Follow these steps to prepare the Windows Vista Start menu:

1. Open the Taskbar and Start Menu Properties dialog box. (Right-click the Start button and choose Properties.)
2. Click the Start Menu tab, if necessary.
3. Set the desired options by un-checking "Store and display a list of recently opened files" and "Store and display a list of recently opened programs."
4. Click the Customize button to open the Customize Start Menu dialog box.
5. Set the desired options by scrolling to the bottom of the list and un-checking "Use large icons." In the "Number of recent programs to display" box, type "0" (zero).
6. Click OK to close the Customize Start Menu dialog box.
7. Click OK to close the Taskbar and Start Menu Properties dialog box.

## *The Screen Saver*

Now, let's discuss the Windows screen saver. If you don't think that enough idle minutes will pass (five, ten, even twenty or more) for it to activate during your presentation, think again. A series of questions or unexpected interruptions can take a lot longer than you might plan for—and you don't want your projected image to suddenly change and become a distraction. And as with the computer desktop, various interesting screen savers—such as photographs, professional artwork, even advertisements for beer or other popular products— can often reflect the personality of the presenter. To keep your audience focused, avoid distracting images like these altogether. Besides, screen savers are virtually unnecessary today. Unlike ten years ago or so, it's almost impossible for an image to damage the computer screen under normal use.

While you're disabling your screen saver, you should also turn off Hibernate mode and set your power options settings to "Never" (if you are using a laptop). Doing so will ensure that your machine doesn't switch to Standby mode after a certain amount of idle time, thus forcing you to enter your user name and password to log back into Windows.

### Disabling Your Screen Saver

To disable your screen saver in Windows Vista, follow these steps:

1. View your desktop. You can practice getting to your desktop quickly by clicking the Show Desktop icon on the Quick Launch toolbar.
2. Right-click anywhere on the desktop and choose Personalize.
3. Click Screen Saver to open the Screen Saver Settings dialog box.
4. Select the desired option by displaying the Screen saver drop-down list and selecting "(None)."
5. Click the "Change power settings" link to display the Control Panel with the power options. (You might need to click the "Show additional plans" link to display "Balanced.")
6. Select "Balanced," and under that selection, click the "Change plan settings" link to display the plan options.
7. From all the drop-down lists, select "Never." These include the "Turn off the display" and "Put the computer to sleep" lists in both the "On battery" and "Plugged in" columns.
8. Click Save changes, and close the Control Panel window.
9. Click OK to close the Screen Saver Settings dialog box.

# Web Browsers

It's now time to move on to your Web browser, such as Internet Explorer, Firefox, Google Chrome, Safari, or others. Because many software applications today are delivered in a Web-based format, chances are, you will demo an online application or Web site at some point.

Most Web browsers include a variety of features designed to help users enhance their experience online. It's important to ensure that these features will work for you and not against you during a product demonstration. For example, I once observed a colleague deliver an online software presentation. Suddenly, while he was answering a question from the audience, a *very* embarrassing instant message from his wife appeared in the corner of the screen. Luckily, the presenter and attendees took it more or less in stride. But he learned a valuable lesson that day about taking the necessary precautions before an online demo.

***Note:*** ***Internet Explorer 8 is used for examples and instructions in this part. If you use another browser, look at its help system to search for the specific steps necessary to customize your browser.***

## *The Home Page*

There may be situations when you must launch Internet Explorer. When that happens, of course, your home page opens automatically.

Which Web address is set for your default home page? I see lots of online demonstrations in which the presenter launches Internet Explorer and a "My Yahoo" type of page appears. Many people customize these pages to display their personal preferences, such as local news, weather, sports, horoscopes, and so forth. One presenter's home page even displayed the performance of his stock portfolio! Although this type of information was useful to him personally, it put him at risk of annoying his audience—or even losing them.

There are many schools of thought in this area. Some presenters recommend setting their own company Web site as the home page, while others lean toward setting it to the Web address of the company they are visiting. But suppose the company you are representing does not have an effective Web site; you might be concerned about "advertising" a second-rate page to your prospect. What if you are demonstrating to a consortium of buyers who are not all members of a single company? How do you choose a page that everyone in the room can relate to?

One solution is to choose a generic home page, such as *www.google.com.* The Google home page is intentionally free of clutter to make it uncomplicated and easy to use. And Google is so widely used, you're not really giving anything away about yourself or your personality by having it as your default site.

## Preparing the Home Page

To set your home page in Internet Explorer 8:

1. Open Internet Explorer, and navigate to the site that you would like to set as your home page (for example, www.google.com).
2. Open the Internet Options dialog box with the General tab active (as shown in the following graphic). One way to do this is to display the Tools menu and choose Internet Options.
3. Under Home Page, click "Use current" to add the current URL as your new home page.
4. Click OK to close the Internet Options dialog box.

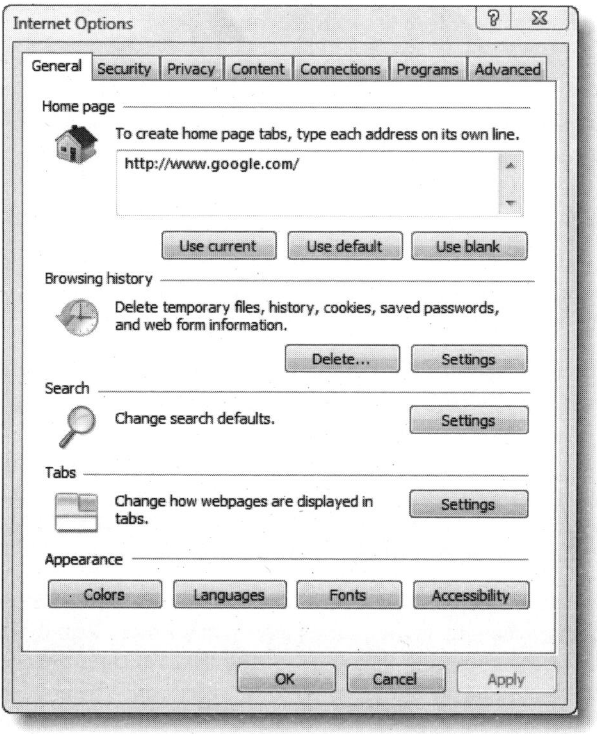


**The Internet Options dialog box**

***Tip:*** ***Internet Explorer allows you to set a blank home page. (In the Internet Options dialog box, under Home Page, click "Use blank.") However, I advise against using this option. Why? Because if your home page is blank, and you start Internet Explorer, there is no obvious way to tell whether you're successfully connected to the Internet. You might not discover there's a problem until you try to navigate to another Web site.***

## *Toolbars*

Most of us are aware that popular search engines such as Google and Yahoo! include their own Internet browser toolbars—and that these toolbars are incredibly easy to install. In fact, they can be difficult to *avoid* installing! Further, many software applications today add shortcuts and mini-toolbars to Internet Explorer as part of their normal installation routines. As a result, many of us have multiple toolbars displayed in our Web browsers. These bars sometimes take up to a *third* of overall screen space and can be as distracting to your online application as a collection of bumper stickers on a new Mercedes.

Following the same philosophy as with the Windows operating system, you should clean house and eliminate all third-party toolbars and other shortcuts in your Internet Explorer browser. I strongly suggest uninstalling Google and similar toolbars from your system completely, as they have a tendency to seemingly reappear on their own.

### Removing Third-Party Toolbars

To delete all of your extraneous toolbars, perform the following steps:

1. Open the Control Panel. (Click the Start button and choose Control Panel.)
2. In the Control Panel, under Programs, click the "Uninstall a program" link to display a list of all programs installed on your computer.
3. Select a program you want to uninstall, such as the Yahoo! toolbar.
4. Click the Uninstall button (located just above the list of programs), and answer all the prompts necessary to complete the uninstall.
5. Repeat steps 3 and 4 for each program you want to uninstall.
6. Close the Control Panel.

### Removing Additional Clutter

In addition to removing third-party toolbars, you can customize the Internet Explorer 8 toolbar. Here's how:

1. Open the Customize Toolbar dialog box. (Click the Tools button on the Command bar and choose Toolbars, Customize.)
2. Customize the current toolbar buttons by using the Add and Remove buttons to include only the buttons you absolutely want in the "Current toolbar buttons" box.
3. Click Close to close the Customize Toolbar dialog box.

The following screen shots underscore the importance of removing clutter in order to emphasize a Web page. Notice how much more real estate is available in the second screen shot.

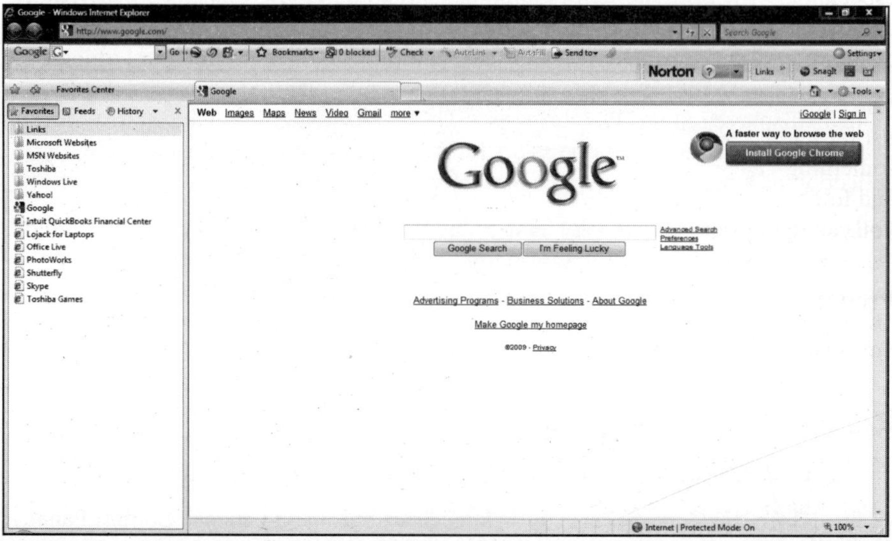

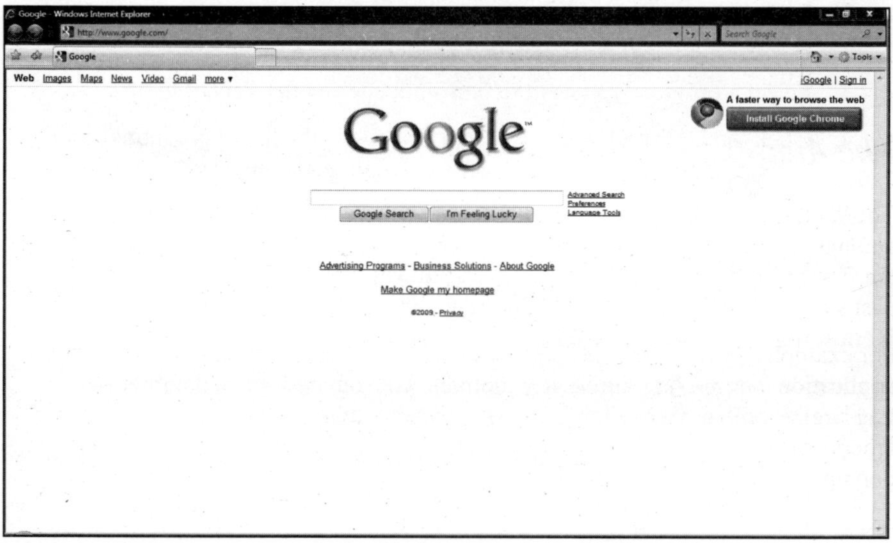

**The second screen is far less distracting**

## The Favorites List

Building a list of often-visited—or favorite—Web pages is awfully convenient, especially when it's important to jump to a site quickly during a presentation. When using a Favorites list, however, you do not want to put personal favorite sites on display for your audience (you're probably noticing a theme here!).

You can easily hide personal sites from public view, while still using the Favorites list for technical presentations. First, create a folder in the Favorites list and name it something generic (for example, "Pages"). Then, move all of your favorite pages and folders to the generic folder. You now have a virtually empty Favorites list, and you can drop your presentation-related favorites into it.

### Preparing the Favorites List

Follow these steps to prepare the Favorites list in Internet Explorer 8:

1. Open the Organize Favorites dialog box. (Click the Favorites button and choose Organize Favorites.)
2. Create a folder by clicking the New Folder button. Enter a generic word to name the folder (such as "Pages").
3. Drag your personal favorite pages and folders into this new folder. Leave your presentation favorites outside of this folder.
4. Click Close to close the Organize Favorites dialog box.

## The Auto-Complete Feature

The "auto-complete" feature in Internet Explorer and other browsers saves time by automatically filling in previously visited Web addresses when you begin entering the first few letters. Although it's convenient, this feature puts you at risk of making past sites you've visited available for public consumption.

For example, let's say you're demonstrating an online computer-aided drafting application from Myso Solutions (a fictional company). During your presentation, you begin entering the address for www.mysoelectronics.com. After you type the letters "m," "y," and "s," the following address, which you've already visited, could pop up:

> http://www.myspace.com/bluehairpartyanimal/blogs.com

Your first objective is to control your audience. You don't want people forming opinions about your online adventures within MySpace.com. To avoid the risk of advertising Web sites you've previously visited, you definitely want to clear your browsing history before your demo.

### Preparing the Auto-Complete Feature

Follow these steps to prepare the auto-complete feature in Internet Explorer 8:

1. Open the Internet Options dialog box with the General tab active. To do so, click Tools and choose Internet Options.
2. Under Browsing History, click Delete to open the Delete Browsing History dialog box.
3. Set the desired options by checking "Temporary Internet files," "Cookies," and "History." Then click Delete.
4. Click OK to close the Internet Options dialog box.

## *Instant Messaging and E-mail Applications*

Finally, to avoid the embarrassment of having personal messages appear on screen, you will disable all instant messaging software (Windows Messenger, Yahoo! Instant Message, etc.), as well as the mail alert in Outlook and similar e-mail applications. Many of us receive e-mail almost constantly throughout the day, from a variety of sources. Besides the distraction of e-mail alerts appearing repeatedly, the subject lines of some messages—especially spam, or junk messages—can be downright offensive.

To disable instant messages and instant e-mail, open each of these applications and choose Options, Preferences, or a similar command. Select the option to turn off visual and audio alerts when messages are received. Better yet, un-check the option to automatically activate the instant messaging program when you turn on your computer.

Your Internet browser is now set so that it displays a disarming, generic home page and is clear of third-party icons and redundant toolbars. You've also guaranteed that your personal information remains personal by clearing your browser history and disabling all instant messaging applications and e-mail alerts. The land mines have been eliminated.

# Other Tools

Every laptop computer includes a touch pad, a keyboard mouse, or some other similar built-in device for moving the pointer. These tools are quite convenient—not to mention essential—when you're working in a limited space, such as on an airplane. But when you're navigating a technical presentation, using a standard hand mouse is a much better idea. Why? Simply put, a mouse gives you far greater navigation control.

Think of the PC gaming environment, where the player must frequently make split-second maneuvers with her pointer or weapon to avoid disaster. Any gamer will tell you that using a standard mouse or other external pointing device is far superior to the built-in touch pad for getting free range of motion. And as far as standard computer usage goes, try clicking and dragging text as quickly with a touch pad as with a regular mouse!

Also, let's face it: many of us get nervous in front of a large group. And when we get nervous, our hands shake ever so slightly. With your fingers shaking on an ultra-sensitive touch pad, it becomes more difficult to navigate in tight areas (for example, placing the cursor between two letters to edit text).

Remember the importance of acting smoothly—no fits or starts. A good optical hand mouse allows us to navigate faster and with more confidence—with far less room for error.

# Part Summary

In this part, you learned how to:

- ▶ Exercise greater audience control and make fewer mechanical errors by organizing your computer.
- ▶ Prepare the Windows Vista operating system by clearing your desktop, optimizing your taskbar and Start menu, and turning off your screen saver.
- ▶ Prepare the Internet Explorer 8 browser by setting the appropriate options for your home page, toolbars, Favorites, auto-complete, instant messaging programs, and e-mail programs.

## ACTION ITEM CHECKLIST

Using the instructions outlined in this part, prepare your computer as if you were planning to deliver a software demonstration tomorrow. Put a check (✓) next to each item as you complete it.

### Windows

**Desktop:**

- ❑ Clear desktop of background images and unnecessary icons and shortcuts.
- ❑ Enable the single-click feature.

**Taskbar:**

- ❑ Disable the auto-hide feature. Anchor the taskbar separately from other windows.
- ❑ Enable the Quick Launch toolbar. Keep only the Show Desktop and Internet Explorer icons.

**Start menu:**

- ❑ Select the option to display small icons.
- ❑ Limit program shortcuts to three or fewer.
- ❑ Empty the My Recent Documents list.

CONTINUED

CONTINUED

**Screen saver:**

- ❑ Disable the screen saver.
- ❑ Disable Hibernate mode.

## Internet Explorer

**Home page:**

- ❑ Set a generic site as your home page.

**Toolbars:**

- ❑ Eliminate all third-party toolbars and shortcuts.
- ❑ Limit the Internet Explorer toolbar to five icons: Back, Forward, Stop, Refresh, and Home.
- ❑ Select the option to display small icons.

**Favorites:**

- ❑ Create a generically named folder and move your personal favorites into that folder.
- ❑ Place presentation-related shortcuts in the main Favorites list.

Auto-complete:

- ❑ Clear the browser history.

Instant messaging and e-mail applications:

- ❑ Disable instant messaging applications.
- ❑ Disable e-mail alerts.

## Other

**Mouse:**

- ❑ Use an optical hand mouse instead of a touch pad or keyboard mouse.

# PART 3

# Delivering Your Demo

*"Virtue is more clearly shown in the performance of fine actions than in the non-performance of base ones."*

**–Aristotle**

## *In this part:*

- ▶ Checking the Equipment
- ▶ Interacting with the Audience
- ▶ Assessing Needs
- ▶ Fielding Questions

# Checking the Equipment

In a perfect world, you will have plenty of setup time in the presentation room before your demo begins. (You can increase the chances of this happening by asking for lead time in your Support and Equipment form.) When setting up, you should do the following:

- Make sure the power strip is on and powering your equipment.
- Test for a live Internet connection.
- Open each application that you will use in your demo.
- Test the projection device, test the connection between the computer and the projector, and make sure the screen resolution is correct on the projection screen.
- Clear your browser history, and then navigate to each page you will demo, if possible (so the pages will load faster during your presentation).
- Test the audio equipment (speakers, microphone).
- Make sure your pen and/or markers have ink.
- Check your flash drive for backup screen shots and/or your PowerPoint presentation.

*Tip:* ***Some audience members filing in might want to strike up a conversation or ask questions when you're setting up. If this happens, politely ask if you can finish your setup first. Time has a habit of accelerating during setup, so you want to make sure everything is functional and in order before interacting with your audience.***

# Interacting with the Audience

If you have time to spare between the setup and your demo, I highly recommend using that time to your advantage by interacting with attendees as they file in. Walk over to say hello to folks and introduce yourself as they find their seats. You'll find that this helps you loosen up, and someone might offer something in conversation that you can use in your demo.

For example, during your presentation, you could refer to a conversation you had with an audience member by offering something like, "Bill, before we got started today, I think you mentioned that a number of computers on your site won't be updated for a year or so, correct? In that case, do you think this lower screen resolution option will help your users?"

You bet it would! What a great way to address a need, and connect with your audience to boot.

Pre-presentation chit-chat is great because it helps you connect with your audience—as well as identify staunch allies and potential grumblers—and prepare accordingly.

## CONNECT WITH YOUR AUDIENCE

What types of questions could you ask that would help you establish a connection with your audience? Write them here:

1. ______________________________

2. ______________________________

3. ______________________________

4. ______________________________

5. ______________________________

# Assessing Needs

Ideally, you have done your homework during the planning phase and involved your audience ahead of time in determining which problem-solving capabilities and end results will be demonstrated. Even so, taking a few moments during the opening to reconfirm the agenda will remind your audience that you are there to address their needs—and not simply to deliver a generic dog-and-pony show. A needs assessment chart also serves as a useful roadmap to keep the demo on track.

## *Creating a Needs Assessment Chart*

To conduct a powerful opening needs assessment, jot down the primary needs that were determined in the planning phase. (Depending on your allotted presentation time, you might want to write these out as part of your setup process.) List each need under a column headed "Issues" or "Needs." Then, create a blank column with the heading "Solutions," as shown in the following table. This column will eventually be filled in with a list of the capabilities (end results) that address each need.

Provide a brief summary of each item. Then ask if there are any other primary concerns that should be added. If additional needs are raised, add them to the bottom of the list, and tell the audience these needs will be covered if time permits. If there is not enough time to cover the additional needs, add these items to your homework list.

### Sequencing Needs

Be sure to list the primary needs in the same order as your plan to demonstrate end results. The sequence of end results should begin with the "second-best" end result first, followed by the third-best, fourth-best, and so on. The last item should be the blue-ribbon-award-winning capability. This last end result should appear on screen at the close of the demo and should stay there throughout the wrap-up.

For example, if your product is planning software for financial organizations, your Needs Assessment list might look something like the chart on the next page:

| Needs | Solutions |
|---|---|
| Need a way to decrease time spent in multiple negotiating meetings throughout the financial quarter | |
| Need to conduct profitability planning up to six months ahead of actual sales | |
| Need to reduce errors made as a result of manually synchronizing data from multiple users who are traveling or telecommuting | |

## *Using the Needs Assessment Chart During the Demo*

The beauty of the Needs Assessment chart is that it helps you stay aligned with your audience's needs and keep the demo on task. Additionally, it gives you the opportunity to map out—in writing—*how* your product addresses each critical need.

Refer to the Needs Assessment chart as you demonstrate each end result. After you have demonstrated an end result, summarize how it addresses the corresponding need, and jot it down in your "Solutions" column. Then, move on to the next need.

After you have demonstrated each end result, your Needs Assessment chart might look something like this:

| Needs | Solutions |
|---|---|
| Need a way to decrease time spent in multiple negotiating meetings throughout the financial quarter | *Feedback Loop* tool enables all stakeholders to communicate in real time |
| Need to conduct profitability planning up to six months ahead of actual sales | New *What-If* scenario modeling feature improves early analytics |
| Need to reduce errors made as a result of manually synchronizing data from multiple users who are traveling or telecommuting | *Offline Mode* enables users to enter forecasting data remotely—and auto-syncs the data when users check in online |

## CREATE A NEEDS ASSESSMENT CHART

Create a Needs Assessment chart for your company's software product by filling in the primary needs of your market and your product's corresponding capabilities (end results) below. Sequence the needs and results so that the second-best result feature is listed first, and the best feature is listed last.

| Needs | Solutions |
|---|---|
| | |
| | |
| | |
| | |
| | |
| | |
| | |

# Fielding Questions

Wouldn't it be wonderful if every audience member asked the ideal question at the perfect time? The good news is that some presentations actually go this way; it's as though you are in one of those 3:00 a.m. infomercials in which each question is teed up perfectly to allow you to segue to the next feature without missing a beat. Perhaps you've been in this situation yourself: A question comes up and is worded in such a way that you can say something like, "I'm so glad you asked that question, because I am pulling up this screen up right now!"

Alas, the bad news is that these occurrences are few and far between. Ill-timed questions, requests to "show me how you do (something that is way off topic)," challenges about programming flaws and bugs, and—worst of all—the smart-aleck who simply takes delight in trying to trip you up are just a few of the many challenges you will face.

There is a real art to fielding questions during a demo. It's not always easy, but believe me, you will get better at it with practice.

Here are some helpful rules of the road for handling questions deftly and professionally.

## *Set Expectations*

Take a few moments up front and share how the Q&A will work. You can say something like:

> *"Please feel free to ask questions along the way, and I will do my best to answer them. But I do want to be respectful of your time, so there may be cases where I ask you to defer a question until I address that topic later on. Finally, if I don't know the answer to a question, I will write it down and promise to e-mail the answer within 24 hours. Sound good?"*

This speech takes only 10 seconds, yet it accomplishes so much. You are acknowledging that your audience's time is valuable. They are now prepped and won't be put off if you put a question on hold. They also won't be disappointed if you can't answer every question then and there. And finally, you are keeping yourself honest by committing to a timely follow-up before the demo even begins.

***Important!*** ***Make sure you are prepared to follow through on your promises. You should have a flip chart (or a legal pad) at the front of the room. When a question comes up that you need to table until later, write it down in one column, and include the name of the person who asked it, if possible. In a second column, record the questions (again, with names) that require research so you can follow up with the group within the promised 24-hour time period. You can name this column "Homework."***

## *Avoid "Prove-It Syndrome"*

Many demonstrators are so proud of their product knowledge that they insist on showing off everything the software can do. Often, these folks hear a simple capability question, immediately start nodding, turn to the computer, and say "Yes, definitely, let me show you how that works." If the capability does not exist, they still start clicking away, and say "Not exactly, but let me show you how to do this. This is just as effective." I call this behavior the "Prove-It Syndrome." A presenter suffering from Prove-It Syndrome exhibits the following symptoms: visible excitement, uncontrollable head-nodding, and the tendency to interrupt and complete other people's questions.

You know this condition is causing wear and tear on the audience when you start hearing people say "You don't have to show me, but can it do _______?"

### Avoiding Prove-It Syndrome

When someone asks you a capability question, follow these steps to avoid Prove-It Syndrome:

1. **Take a breath.** Before you do anything else, take a breath and treat your brain to some oxygen. In that tiny space of time, you will allow yourself to think about the question, and allow the rest of the audience to hear it.
2. **Repeat the question.** "So let me restate your question to make sure I understand it. You would like to know whether the system will enable your department to run a delinquent payee report sorted by invoice after each fiscal quarter; is that correct?"
3. **Just answer the question!** A simple "Yes" or "No" will do in most cases—without Proving It. You'll be able to tell by the person's facial expression if a one-word response is not enough. Of course, you can always add some of your own personality. I like to use some humor. For example, "Now that is a great question—and one of my personal favorites. Why? Because the answer is a resounding yes!"

## *Stick to the Agenda*

Yes, listening to your audience members' needs is crucial. Yes, you want to answer their questions and help them understand if they are confused. **But *you* own this demo.** Your agenda was determined in concert with the customer ahead of time. Your customer told you what the company's needs were in the planning phase, and based on those needs, you decided—*as a team*—what the demo would cover. You even reconfirmed the agenda at the opening of the presentation and made modifications as necessary.

Staying out of the rabbit hole means respecting your audience by sticking to the overall agenda. Of course, there will be instances when it benefits the group to temporarily veer from the script and quickly get back on task. You're allowed to think on your feet and be flexible. But there will also be situations when someone asks you to show a feature or process that is way off topic or that would take way too much time to demonstrate. When this happens, many demonstrators (particularly those suffering from Prove-It Syndrome) dive right in without thinking—"Yessiree, I sure can show you that! Here we go!"—and take the group down a rabbit hole of functionality that leads to more and more questions. Before you know it, the other attendees are shifting uncomfortably in their seats, looking at their shoes, having side conversations, or checking their watches. It is very difficult to recover once you've fallen into this predicament.

### Staying Out of the Rabbit Hole

It's easy to stay out of the rabbit hole if you follow these steps:

1. Take a breath.
2. Repeat the question. This is critical because by repeating it, you will subtly reinforce how off-topic the question is. The person who asked it will be singled out, but he won't necessarily know it.
3. Remind the person that you want to respect everyone's time and defer the question until after the session.

For example, the scene could work like this:

**Presenter:** *(take a breath)* "OK, I heard a few questions there! Let me make sure I understand them. You want to look at the list of file formats that the personnel reports can be saved in, you'd like to see me save a sample result report in Excel format, and you want to see that file imported into the management platform. Is that right?"
*(Other audience members roll their eyes.)*

**Attendee:** "Uh, yes. Please."

**Presenter:** "I'm happy to show you these steps, but I do want to be respectful of everyone's time. Would it be OK if I write this one down and we hold it until later? I've blocked out a few minutes after the session so I can show more detailed functionality—and anyone who would like to can stay and see our new reporting features. Would that be fair to everyone?"

**Attendee:** "Sounds good, sure."

By saying that you want to be "respectful of everyone's time" and "fair to everyone," you put the group on your side and minimize the chance of the individual's digging his heels in. The head honcho in the audience might even help you out and say "Yes, let's move on."

## *Don't Guess at Answers*

Like it or not, some people in the audience will look upon you as the sage of all things technical during your demo. After all, you're supposed to be the product person, right? So it's easy to see why many presenters are tempted to guess at answers they are not 100% sure about.

If you don't know the answer to a product question, admit it! You can say something like: "You know, I'm not 100% sure of the answer to that question, and I don't want to give you incorrect information. Let me write it down, and I'll be sure to get back to you with the correct answer within 24 hours." Jot it down in the Homework column on your flip chart or in your notebook, along with the name of the person asking the question.

Your audience should appreciate the honesty. The last thing you want to do is lose the account because you winged it and gave the wrong information

***Tip:*** ***Make a deal if a colleague is visiting or co-presenting with you: If an "I don't know" question comes up during the final 10 minutes of the demo, the colleague will send an e-mail message (from his Blackberry or similar device) to the product expert. If the expert is in the office and checking e-mail, you might be able to provide an answer immediately.*** **Make sure, however, to use this strategy in only the final 10 minutes.** ***Otherwise, the audience might expect you to e-mail any and every question back to the home office during the demo.***

## *Understand Roles and Responsibilities*

As a sales professional, you're trained to help provide solutions to problems. And as you become more familiar with whatever software you are selling, there is a real temptation to be the product person in every sense of the term. For example, if you observe that many customers are making the same error, you might be tempted to play the part of Technical Support Rep and demonstrate how to avoid the error during your demo.

You must walk a fine line between helping your customers yourself and turning problems and questions over to the real experts. The danger in positioning yourself as Product Expert vs. Sales Rep is that customers could begin coming to you for everything; this, of course, would put you at risk of providing bad information and spending time supporting when you should be selling.

Make sure to direct potential and existing customers to the appropriate channels. For example: user questions should go through tech support; feedback should be sent to marketing; bugs should be entered in the product Web page; and so on.

# *Turn that Frown Upside-Down*

Many of my clients regularly give follow-on demonstrations to current customers on a regular basis. The software is either a new release, an add-on solution to the main product, or a new tool altogether. These demonstrators tell me they are often challenged by one or more disenchanted or irate users in the audience. Perhaps somebody applied the product incorrectly and got frustrated, encountered bugs, or voted against buying the solution in the first place. Whatever the reason, he takes his aggravation out on the presenter.

It's not always easy to stay positive when you're getting pelted with bullets of negativity. But you must not get flustered, show your frustration, or become confrontational. Likewise, don't negotiate with the intent of getting the person "on your side." Doing so is pretty transparent in a group setting and is often a fruitless effort.

Instead, really listen to what the person says, and give him the benefit of the doubt. After all, every software product has bugs, and not everyone can be a power user. As you listen to him, tell yourself that you honestly want to help solve his problem, but without taking the group down the rabbit hole.

## User Errors

If the complaint is about a perceived flaw that is actually caused by user errors, do not correct the person or tell him that he's using the product incorrectly. You'll do better to put the person in good company rather than calling him out on the carpet. For example, you could say, "I'm glad you raised that point, because I've heard the same thing from other customers recently. It seems that our user interface is a bit confusing on that series of screens. I've brought this up with our design team to see how we can simplify the interface. So thank you for mentioning it."

## Legitimate Bugs

If the complaint is about a legitimate bug in the software, acknowledge the bug, write it down, and ask if the person is willing to stay for a few minutes after the session to describe it in more detail or even show an example. Most users who find bugs love to show what they uncovered. Taking this approach not only diffuses the situation, but it also enables you to partner with the person and perhaps enlist him to get involved in user testing.

## *Don't Forget Your Deferred and Homework Questions*

During your demo, you most likely parked a number of deferred and homework questions on your flip chart.

### The Deferred Column

Here's how to handle the deferred questions:

1. Address each question at the appropriate time. This will require you to keep an eye on the chart as you transition to each topic.
2. Use the person's name when you answer. "Ken, you asked about the minimum system requirements earlier, is that correct? Here they are...."
3. Place a checkmark next to each question after it is answered.
4. During wrap-up, answer any remaining questions that are not checked.

### The Homework Column

Here's how to handle the homework questions:

1. Re-read each question aloud, and ask the group if you missed anything.
2. Remind the audience that you will e-mail answers to the group within 24 hours.

# Part Summary

In this part, you learned how to:

- Check your presentation equipment while minimizing audience interruptions.
- Establish a connection and rapport with your audience before the demo begins.
- Stay aligned with your audience and their needs by creating a Needs Assessment chart.
- Field a variety of questions with an eye toward keeping your demo on track and within the allotted time.

# PART 4

# Demo Techniques and Style

*"I've learned that people will forget what you said, people will forget what you did, but people will never forget how you made them feel."*

**–Maya Angelou**

## *In this part:*

- ▶ Navigating Like a Pro
- ▶ Logging In and Typing
- ▶ Mouse vs. Keyboard Shortcuts
- ▶ Presentation Techniques

# Navigating Like a Pro

Whenever you catch the weather report on the 6 o'clock evening news, you're observing a first-rate software demo in action. Watch the meteorologist closely, and you'll see that he's controlling the interactive weather map with a small electronic device in one hand. This device has various buttons that allow him to zoom in on particular locations, display complex weather patterns, change from map to satellite view, and more, all with a few clicks of his thumb or forefinger. Of course, you're probably not paying attention to the remote control—your eyes are most likely moving between the map and his face, depending on what he's talking about.

How effective would it be if the meteorologist stood anchored in one spot, and kept pausing to look down and make sure he was clicking the right button? Or worse, what if he methodically described each action he made? For example:

> **Meteorologist:** "All right, I am now going to click the left button on my remote control. In a moment, we should see the high temperatures in the metro area. There it goes. Now, I'll press the top button and this will display tomorrow's forecast."

Of course, this never happens. If it did, that meteorologist would be looking for another line of work, and fast. The meteorologist's presentation style is effective, not only because he comes across as an expert on his subject, but also because his delivery is clean and entertaining. He keeps you more or less interested without distracting from the screen or getting in the way.

Likewise, a great software presenter never gets in the way of his product. Throughout the following pages, you'll learn valuable tips on controlling your equipment and refining your presentation style in ways that make you look like an expert while making your demo run as smooth as silk.

# Logging In and Typing

Think back to a software demonstration in which you had to type information on the keyboard to show a particular feature. Did your hands shake? Did you make more typos than you normally would if you were sitting alone at your desk? Did you have to start again because you mistyped something and the software didn't do what it was supposed to?

The next time you observe a software demo, watch carefully when the presenter types information. Unless she's world typing champion Barbara Blackburn, chances are she will make at least one typo. She also might not speak as smoothly when she's typing. This is understandable because typing requires a certain degree of concentration.

## *Prepare for Easy Typing*

The best software presenters avoid typing words and sentences whenever possible during a demo. But some typing is almost always necessary. For example, demonstrators must usually log into whatever product they're showing by typing a user name and password. Depending on the complexity of the product, you might even have to log in multiple times, using different user names and passwords throughout the demo—which means more typing. To further complicate matters, many products today require the user name to be in e-mail syntax, which requires a minimum number of characters, as well as the "@" and "." characters.

Unfortunately, scores of demonstrations never really get off the ground because the presenter mistypes his account information and gets an error message, or because he forgets a user name or password entirely and has to look around for the right information.

You may also have observed otherwise serious demonstrations that are trivialized because the presenter uses the names of entertainers, political figures, professional athletes, or worst of all, *cartoon characters* for his sample accounts. Suppose that you are presenting a sophisticated and high-priced product solution to a room full of executives. These people are responsible for spending thousands or even millions of dollars of their companies' money. Put yourself in their position. What would you think about a salesperson if he logged into his product with the user name donald.duck@mycompany.com? At the very least, wouldn't you think twice about his professionalism?

## Creating a User Name and Password System

You should incorporate a user name and password system that allows you to:

- Log in fast every time, without notes and without hesitation.
- Ensure that your account names are professional and non-distracting.
- Use e-mail syntax without using someone else's actual e-mail address.
- Have plenty of backup accounts if there is a problem with your primary account.

Here's a user name and password system that meets those objectives:

- **Use the first and last names of people in your company.** In fact, use the names of people in your department, if possible. These are the folks with whom you interact most frequently, so you should be able to recall their names easily. However, to minimize the chance of mistyping, avoid including long names.
- **Create a realistic—but fictional—e-mail address for each account.** To do this, simply add the last four digits of your own phone number to the user portion of the address. For example, use "sue.brock7277@crisp.com" as opposed to "sue.brock@crisp.com" (that user name is for the real Sue Brock!). Each address should be in this format.
- **Make each password identical and something you will not forget,** but not the password you use for your own private and sensitive information.

The following table includes 15 sample user accounts that use this user name and password system.

| First Name | Last Name | User Name | Password |
|---|---|---|---|
| Phil | Bozek | phil.bozek7277@crisp.com | pencil |
| Sue | Brock | sue.brock7277@crisp.com | pencil |
| Rick | Conlow | rick.conlow7277@crisp.com | pencil |
| Bert | Decker | bert.decker7277@crisp.com | pencil |
| Kay | DuPont | kay.dupont7277@crisp.com | pencil |
| Dan | Feldman | dan.feldman7277@crisp.com | pencil |
| Lloyd | Finch | lloyd.finch7277@crisp.com | pencil |
| Elvin | Haynes | elvin.haynes7277@crisp.com | pencil |
| Herb | Kindler | herb.kindler7277@crisp.com | pencil |
| Steve | Mandel | steve.mandel7277@crisp.com | pencil |
| Bill | Martin | bill.martin7277@crisp.com | pencil |
| Wil | McKnight | wil.mcknight7277@crisp.com | pencil |
| Rebecca | Morgan | rebecca.morgan7277@crisp.com | pencil |
| Cynthia | Scott | cynthia.scott7277@crisp.com | pencil |
| Gordon | Shea | gordon.shea7277@crisp.com | pencil |

Now you have a stockpile of sample accounts and names that look authentic, are easy to recall, and don't distract from your demo.

## CREATE SAMPLE USER ACCOUNTS

Using the system outlined on the previous pages, take a few minutes to create 15 sample user accounts for your software product.

| First Name | Last Name | User Name | Password |
|---|---|---|---|
| | | | |
| | | | |
| | | | |
| | | | |
| | | | |
| | | | |
| | | | |
| | | | |
| | | | |
| | | | |
| | | | |
| | | | |
| | | | |
| | | | |
| | | | |

## Practicing the Login Process

After you create your sample account list, practice logging into your product with each name so you can be sure you created each account correctly. There might be one or two names that you find difficult to type. If so, replace them with other names of people you work with.

Another important reason for logging in beforehand: most products include a license agreement and other welcome screens for first-time users. The time to acknowledge these first-time-user screens is not during your demonstration.

As I mentioned previously, you might have to log in multiple times under different accounts during a single demo, or you might need to log in only once, with one account. It all depends on the complexity of the product or how much functionality you want to show. Either way, you will most likely have to log in at least once. So how do you avoid making typographical errors during your initial login when everyone is watching?

You *could* log in before the presentation. Some presenters log into their product as part of their setup so they don't have to type in front of the audience and risk a mistake. In fact, I used to take this approach myself. However, I soon realized that many people wanted to see me log in so they could be sure that it was an easy process. That's fair.

## Logging In During Your Demo

Here's a great way to show the login process and avoid making typos at the same time:

1. Perform your normal demo setup:
    a. Display the login screen and enter your user name.
    b. Copy the user name to the Clipboard. (Press Ctrl+A to select the text, and then press Ctrl+C to copy the text.)
    c. Press Tab to navigate to the password field.
    d. Enter the password.
    e. Verify that you can log in successfully.
    f. Log out of the software.
    g Display the login screen, and place the insertion point in the user name field.

2. During your demo, perform the following steps:
    a. Paste the user name by pressing Ctrl+V (typing avoided!).
    b. Press Tab to move the insertion point to the password field.
    c. Enter the password (remember, you should have an easy-to-recall and easy-to-type word, such as "pencil").
    d. Log in, and begin your demo.

With this method, the only word you will type is "pencil." And believe me, due to the sheer repetition of using this password for all of your accounts, you will type it correctly almost 100% of the time.

## Login Practice

Using the steps on the previous page, practice logging into your product with one of your 15 new sample user accounts. Practice repeatedly until it becomes automatic. Then practice the steps under a second account. These will be your two primary user accounts during your next actual demo.

# Mouse vs. Keyboard Shortcuts

There is a fine line between delivering a demo that's smooth and sure, and alienating your audience by moving so fast that they can't keep up with you. On the one hand, if you use keyboard shortcuts, you're going to get around your application efficiently, making the software look faster. On the other hand, by not showing your audience how you accomplish something, people might get confused or think the product is difficult to use.

What to do? The answer depends largely on your audience. If you are demonstrating to potential users who are mostly unfamiliar with computers, you might need to convince them that your product is user-friendly. A mouse is the better approach here; you can show them how you are getting from point A to point B, and even describe your actions for reinforcement. Be aware of your pace and timing, however. Your normal speed might result in the mouse pointer moving so fast that it will be distracting. Slow it down.

If you are showing your product to computer experts (particularly self-proclaimed ones!), you will be spending more time focusing on what the software accomplishes, rather than on how to get there. These are the situations in which I might use more keyboard shortcuts to keep up the pace and avoid the distraction of constantly reaching for my mouse.

## *Common Keyboard Shortcuts*

Here is a list of common keyboard shortcuts that will help you navigate your demo faster:

- **Ctrl+C:** Copy.
- **Ctrl+X:** Cut.
- **Ctrl+V:** Paste.
- **Ctrl+Z:** Undo. Use this faster, more subtle command instead of backspacing over a mistake.
- **Ctrl+Y:** Redo.
- **Ctrl+F:** Find text. This is particularly helpful if you are demonstrating a screen with a lot of text and need to quickly navigate to a specific point.
- **Ctrl+A:** Select all text.
- **Ctrl+P:** Print.
- **Ctrl+N:** New. In Internet Explorer, this command opens an identical Web page in a new browser window.
- **Ctrl+Home:** Move to the first character of a document or to the top of a Web page.
- **Ctrl+End:** Move to the last character of a document or to the bottom of a Web page. Beats using the scrollbar every time!
- **Alt+Tab:** Switch between open programs. Great if you are running a PowerPoint slide show and your product simultaneously.
- **Tab, and then Enter:** On a Web page, pressing Tab selects the next object, and then pressing Enter activates that object. This is an excellent command to use with the mouse. For example, if you are demonstrating an online exam, you could answer a question by selecting an option with your mouse, press Tab to move the focus to the "next question" link, and press Enter to activate the link, which will display the next question.

## *Keyboard Shortcuts to Navigate in PowerPoint*

When it comes to PowerPoint, less is more. Use it sparingly, if at all. Frankly, if you have done a thorough job of understanding your prospects' needs and setting expectations beforehand, there should be no need for the usual PowerPoint presentation. That said, many audiences have become so used to PowerPoint that they might feel like something is missing without at least a few introductory slides to frame the demonstration and introduce the product. So be it. And of course, there will be situations when disaster strikes and you find yourself without an Internet connection. In such instances, having a collection of screen shots saved in a PowerPoint presentation is essential.

### Do's and Don'ts

So if you plan to use PowerPoint, don't let it usurp your audience. Make PowerPoint work for you by remembering the following navigational *Do's* and *Don'ts*.

- When switching back and forth between PowerPoint and your product:
  - ***Do*** use Alt+Tab to switch between applications.
  - ***Don't*** shut down and re-open PowerPoint.
- When the presentation is displayed in Slide Show view and you want to temporarily black out the projection:
  - ***Do*** hit the "W" or "B" key. This turns the screen white or black. Subsequently pressing any key will make the slide reappear.
  - ***Don't*** turn off the projector or (even worse) place a book in front of the projector.
- When you want to move to the next slide (or return to the previous slide):
  - ***Do*** hit the Up and Down arrows on your keyboard.
  - ***Don't*** use those faded-out icons on the bottom-left corner of the slide, or right-click. Both actions are distracting to the audience.
- When the presentation is in Normal or Slide Sorter view and you want to resume in Slide Show view from a particular slide:
  - ***Do*** make sure the appropriate slide is selected, and click the Slide Show icon or press Shift+F5.
  - ***Don't*** panic and hit the "From Beginning" button. This will bring you back to Slide #1 in Slide Show view. There is nothing more annoying than watching a presenter shuffle through a dozen previously viewed slides to get back to his place.

# Presentation Style

You may have heard the saying, "It's not what you say, it's how you say it." Well, in the context of delivering a great software demonstration that is honest, informative, engaging, and buy-worthy, you might rephrase this expression: "It's what you say, and it's how you say it (oh, and try not to stand in front of the projector)!"

There are hundreds of books that teach effective presentation skills. And certainly, incorporating tried and true presentation techniques is a critical part of any good software demo. But there are other stylistic elements that should be considered when you're presenting software and encouraging your audience to buy it. We will explore these elements—right down to what you have in your pockets—over the next few pages.

## *Using Lists and Numbers*

The next time you find yourself waiting in line at the supermarket, take a look at the magazines on display in the checkout aisle. You will most likely find at least one or two "list" headlines on each cover. Here are some examples:

- **Seven** ways to improve your relationship
- Eliminate debt in **five** easy steps
- **34** restaurants to visit on your cross-country escape
- **Twelve** killer ab workouts to prepare you for beach season!

List headlines are a time-tested strategy for capturing readers' attention. People respond favorably to lists; our brains tend to process lists more easily than non-linear information, and data that is presented in a list can be recalled more easily.

To help make important product capabilities memorable, try using lists and numbers as part of your demos. Keep your lists on the short side (five items or fewer) so the information can be processed more easily. Finally, by inserting a brief pause before introducing your list, you increase the likelihood of your audience taking notes.

Here are a couple of examples of how you can incorporate lists and numbers into your presentation:

**Instead of:** "The frequency analysis report saves me time because I don't have to enter redundant information."

**Say this:** "Here are *three key ways* I save time by using the frequency analysis report *(pause)*. First…"

**Instead of:** "We've greatly enhanced our calendar interface based on user feedback."

**Say this:** "Here are the *top five enhancements* we made in our calendar interface, based on customer feedback *(pause)*. Number one…"

## CREATE LIST HEADLINES

Write a list headline with corresponding benefits for a popular feature of your product. An example is provided for you.

### Example:

Product feature: Frequency analysis report

List headline: Three ways the frequency analysis report saves time

Corresponding benefits:

1. I can see user and result information in one area without having to pull multiple reports.
2. Custom filters enable me to export quarterly exam summaries in one step.
3. I can now analyze trends without having to look at individual user results.

### Your turn:

Product feature: ____________________________________________

____________________________________________________________

List headline: ______________________________________________

____________________________________________________________

Corresponding benefits:

1. __________________________________________________________

   __________________________________________________________

2. __________________________________________________________

   __________________________________________________________

3. __________________________________________________________

   __________________________________________________________

## *Dealing with the Competition*

In most cases, your software will be evaluated against other competitive products. In fact, many customers schedule multiple vendors to demo their products on the same day, so it's not uncommon to run into your competition in the hallway or the waiting area.

Salespeople are often trained to spotlight particular product features that are superior to the competition's. This is a great approach, provided that those features address the customer's primary needs, but comparing your solution to competitive products is tricky. How do you ensure that the audience gets the message without bashing the other vendors?

### The Green Light

The good news is that the customer will sometimes give you the green light. If the need is serious enough that the feature will make or break the success of the buyer, the customer might simply ask:

**Customer:** "This feature is very important to us, so can you tell me how it works better in your product than what we've seen in Product Y?"

In this case, you can answer the question directly, but you still need to be tactful. For example, you might respond with something like:

**Presenter:** "Well, I'm by no means an expert on Product Y, but I have met some users with a similar need as yours. These folks tell me that our feature (describe what it does better than Product Y)."

If you don't get the green light, but highlighting the superiority of your product feature is crucial to the sale, then it's up to you to communicate it in a responsible, respectful way. If you are absolutely positive that your feature is better than Product Y's feature, you can put the customer in charge of getting your competition to admit it! Here's how:

## Highlighting the Superiority of Your Product

During your demonstration, get your audience to confirm how important your superior feature is. Really get people to nod their heads and admit that they cannot be successful unless the feature works the way it will operate in your product. Then put on your consultant hat, and advise them of what questions to ask the competing demonstrator so they (the customer) can be sure that their critical need is being addressed. The goal is to get the customer to word the questions in such a way that the competing rep has to admit that his product feature is inferior to yours. For example:

**Presenter:** "Based on what you've told me, it sounds as though you need this feature to do A, B, and C; is that correct? In fact, I'm hearing that if the product does not accomplish these three specific tasks, your problem is not really going to get solved. Is that fair?

OK, if you are looking at other products as part of your decision-making process, we're in agreement that you've got to be sure those products include a feature that can accomplish A, B, and C. If I were in your position and evaluating product options, here are a few questions I might ask a vendor, to make sure the product addresses your three critical needs…"

Your audience will most likely jot down the questions you suggest, so word them carefully. Don't suggest Yes/No questions. Instead, suggest questions that begin with "how," so the demonstrator will be forced to explain the inferior capability in detail.

Remember, though: you must be 100% positive that your feature is superior for this strategy to work!

## COMPETITION QUESTIONS

Consider a capability of your product that you are 100% certain is superior to the competition's. If the competing rep were showing you his product, what questions could you ask that would require him to expose the feature's inferiority in detail? Write them below.

1. ______________________________________________
______________________________________________?

2. ______________________________________________
______________________________________________?

3. ______________________________________________
______________________________________________?

4. ______________________________________________
______________________________________________?

5. ______________________________________________
______________________________________________?

## *Dealing with Page Delays*

Ever click a link in a product demo, and wait, and wait for the next page to load? When this happens, the room becomes eerily silent, doesn't it? Someone coughs. Still waiting. Is this page going to load, or what? Let me click again. Nothing. Wait—here it comes. Whew! OK, back to business. "As I was saying…," you continue….

No real harm done. But it would be nice to keep the overall presentation running smoothly if and when you encounter the occasional page delay. Here are three simple strategies:

- **Delay Strategy 1: Describe what will happen on the next page.** Let the page interrupt you when it loads, quickly recap what you described before the interruption, and continue. For example:

    a. "So I simply click the OK button…" Screen delay.

    b. "… and when the screen appears, I should see a list that includes the first and last names of each user who created an entry between January 1 and today. Now, there are three ways I can use this data to save time. First, I can…" And the screen advances.

    c. "…and there it is—OK, here's the data I was describing: names and dates in these columns. So I'm going to save time in three ways. Number one…"

- **Delay Strategy 2: Acknowledge the delay and ask a question.** Let the discussion wrap up, and continue. For example:

    a. "So I simply click the OK button…" Screen delay.

    b. "While this page is loading, let me ask to see a show of hands: how many of you can see yourselves creating monthly reports? And annual reports? Kevin, what would be the benefit of running monthly vs. annual data in your case?" And the screen advances.

    c. After Kevin answers, you continue with the demo, "Here we see a list that includes the first and last names of each user who created an entry between January 1 and today."

- **Delay Strategy 3:Use humor, but sparingly.** For example:

    a. "So I simply click the OK button…" Screen delay.

    b. "It's come to my attention that this screen moves more slowly when everyone is looking at it. Kind of like a watched pot never boils, sort of thing. So, if you could kindly turn away… "And the screen advances.

    c. "There we go. Let's remember that rule for the next time!"

## *Clothing Tips*

When dressing for your demonstration, keep the following tips in mind:

- **Avoid bulky wristwatches.** They make typing more difficult. Same goes for dangling bracelets, which also clatter pretty loudly against the keyboard.
- **Wear a tie clip** to prevent your necktie from getting in the way of the keyboard or brushing against the touchpad.
- **Shed the blazer or suit jacket**, if you can get away with it. Both restrict your movement when reaching for the mouse or referring to something on screen.
- **Wear flat shoes** instead of high heels to make moving between the computer and screen easier.
- **Remove the name tag from around your neck** when presenting at a conference or trade show. Not only do name tags get in the way of the keyboard when you bend over to type, but they are usually encased in plastic, which can cause a distraction by reflecting light back onto the audience.
- **Empty your pockets.** Remove coins, keys, and other jangling materials.

## *Positioning and Movement*

When giving your presentation, try to plan your positioning in the room and how you'll move around during your demo. The following list offers some factors to consider:

- **Put the computer and projector on separate tables** if you can arrange it. This will give you more room to maneuver the mouse, and you won't be as likely to bump the projector.
- **Carry a three-ring binder with you.** That way, if you must use your laptop on a slanted podium, you can level the surface with the binder and prevent the mouse from constantly sliding down.
- **Position the laptop so that you are facing the attendees when using the keyboard or mouse.** You never want to turn your back to the audience!
- **Avoid sitting down when operating the computer**, if possible. Make sure your audience can always see you.
- **Make sure the laptop is not partially blocking the projector**, and that *you* do not block it when operating the laptop.
- **Avoid passing between the projector and projection screen**, especially if you're like me and move around a lot.
- **If you gesture toward the projection screen to emphasize a particular part of the interface, stand to the side and do not actually touch the screen.** Doing so could result in it tipping over or accidentally rolling up like a window shade.
- **Keep some electrical tape with you so you can tape down any cords that are in your path.** You don't want to trip over a power cord.

# Part Summary

In this part, you learned how to:

- Incorporate shortcuts and work-arounds to make your demos look better and run more smoothly.
- Build a user name and password system that enables you to get your demo off to a good start.
- Navigate in PowerPoint so that it does not get in the way of the software you are demonstrating.
- Utilize presentation techniques, competitive strategies, and delivery tips that add style to your demos.

# PART 5

# Conducting Remote Demos

> *Extraordinary creature! So close a friend, and yet so remote."*
>
> **–Thomas Mann**

## *In this part:*

- ▶ Web Conferencing Applications
- ▶ Tips and Tricks for Conducting a Successful Remote Demo

# Web Conferencing Applications

As Internet technology continues to advance—and travel budgets continue to tighten—Web conferencing software is becoming increasingly popular. Web conferencing software (also called *desktop sharing* or *online meeting* software) includes such programs as WebEx, GoToMeeting, and Microsoft Office Live Meeting. Web conferencing allows anyone with a browser and a live Internet connection to meet and collaborate in real time. Besides being used for collaborative meetings, presentations, and training sessions, Web conferencing technology is particular useful for delivering software demonstrations to remote audiences.

Using a Web conferencing platform, you can give a remote demonstration to one attendee or a hundred. You might present to a group where all the attendees are in the same room (the group might hook up one machine to a projection device so everyone can watch the same screen, for example), or you could present to audience members who are scattered throughout the country or the world. Each attendee is watching your demo from his or her own computer while listening on the telephone. Most Web conferencing packages even allow you to record the meeting, enabling you to e-mail it to customers or post it to a Web page later.

A basic Web conference is illustrated below.

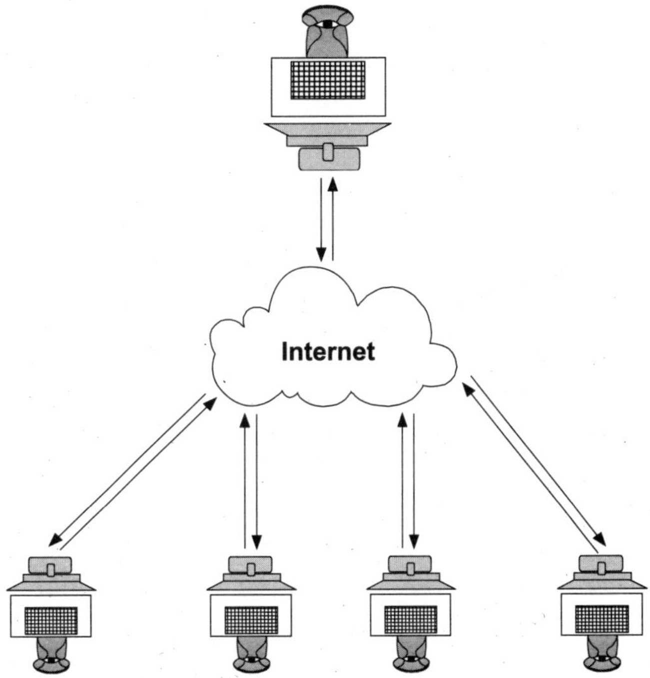


**A Web conference**

## How Do Most Web Conferencing Applications Work?

Following these basic steps, you'll be able to use most Web conferencing applications:

1. **Schedule the meeting.** The meeting host sets up a meeting in the software by using controls that enable her to schedule it for a specific date and time.
2. **Invite the participants.** The host invites participants to the meeting via an automatically generated e-mail message or by sending her own separate e-mail message. The message contains the information needed to join the meeting, such as meeting date and time, URL, password, teleconference, and login instructions. The message also includes instructions for downloading and installing a small software applet, if such software is needed to participate.
3. **Invitees log in.** On the day of the meeting, invitees join it by logging in and calling in to the teleconference.
4. **Give the demonstration.** The host uses tools such as a whiteboard, drawing tools, and desktop sharing capabilities to collaborate with attendees.
5. **Discussions take place** via the conference call and the Web conference's chat area.
6. **Log out.** At the end of the demo, the host and participants hang up and log out of the Web conferencing application .

When used correctly, a software demo delivered remotely via Web conferencing can be just as effective as an in-the-flesh presentation. That said, try to keep the old Spider-Man credo in mind when planning a remote demo: "With great power comes great responsibility!"

## Why Do Some Remote Demos Fail?

What could go wrong in a remote demo? Well, plenty. For one thing, your demo is dead in the water if your Internet connection suddenly goes out. If disaster strikes during a face-to-face demo, you can always rely on other strategies (screen shots or offline Web pages stored in the cache), but in a remote environment, the presentation depends entirely on a live (preferably high-speed) Internet connection. Without an Internet connection, there is no demo!

## Describe Your Experience

List some potential problems that you think could occur in a remote demonstration or that have occurred in a remote demo that you attended or hosted. Compare your answers with the list that follows this exercise.

1. ______________________________________________

   ______________________________________________

2. ______________________________________________

   ______________________________________________

3. ______________________________________________

   ______________________________________________

4. ______________________________________________

   ______________________________________________

### Common Problems

Here's a list of some reasons that remote demos can fail:

- Sudden loss of Internet connection.
- Login problems. Attendees have difficulty logging into and/or downloading the necessary meeting software.
- Lag time. Internet speed varies among audience members, resulting in lag time between your actions and what audience members see on screen.
- Distracting background noise coming from one or more attendees' locations.
- Miscommunication. You might be unaware that you're moving too fast—or too slow—because of the inability to read facial expressions.

The list goes on. While Web conferencing uses cool technology, it's often the technology itself that can trip you up and negatively affect your demo (and jeopardize the sale). It's up to you, therefore, to obsessively prepare for anything and everything that could possibly go wrong. You've got to be on your toes. "With great power comes great responsibility," my friend!

# Tips and Tricks for Conducting a Successful Remote Demo

Most companies today license a particular Web conferencing service for their employees, but you might be free to choose your own. Either way, stick with one application and devote a significant amount of time to mastering it. Many services include useful documentation, video tutorials, and in-person training. Make use of everything you can.

That said, try to avoid the fancier, bell-and-whistle features that could make using the software more complex for you and your audience. Stick to the basics: meeting scheduling, desktop sharing, and simple communication. Sure, you could use the instant polling feature, but some audience members might not appreciate taking a survey when all they really want to do is learn how your product can help them. Plus, the more you (and they) have to do, the greater the risk of problems occurring.

## *Limit the Number of Attendees*

Even though there is a real cost benefit in being able to present to hundreds of participants in one shot, you would do well to place a cap on the number of attendees. Limit attendance to 20 participants or fewer. Keeping attendance on the low side enables you to more easily engage with your audience and encourage them to participate. In addition, some attendees *will* have trouble logging in, seeing your desktop, or figuring out how to juggle the presentation with the other applications they are running. If just 5% of the attendees in a 300-person meeting have technical difficulties, that's 15 people you have to help before the demo even begins.

## *Send Your Own Meeting Instructions*

Your Web conferencing application most likely includes a feature that automatically e-mails participants with login instructions after you schedule the meeting. But attendees are more likely to pay attention to the instructions if you send them personally. Also, sometimes the automatically generated message included in many packages is not explicit enough.

A sample letter with meeting instructions is on the next page.

# ONLINE MEETING INSTRUCTIONS

To: Paul Smith
From: Steve Anyrep
Date: October 8, 2012
Subject: Online Meeting Instructions

I hope you're looking forward to next week's online meeting. The purpose of this e-mail message is to confirm the meeting schedule and provide you with additional details to ensure that our session exceeds your expectations.

| | |
|---|---|
| Meeting Title: | How to Increase Productivity with Product X |
| Meeting Date: | Monday, October 15, 2012 |
| Start Time: | 3:00 PM ET |
| End Time: | 4:00 PM ET |

IMPORTANT: Please take a few minutes to follow these steps, no later than Thursday, October 11.

1. Register online at *<insert link to meeting URL>*.
2. Download and install the meeting manager software applet at *<insert link to software download area>*.
3. Send a confirmation e-mail message to *<insert your e-mail address>* with "Steps Completed" in the Subject line. No message body text is required.

To start the online meeting:

1. Go to *<insert link to meeting URL>*.
2. Log into your account.
3. Click "Start Now."
4. Follow the instructions that appear on your screen.

Teleconference information:

Dial-in number: 1-888-555-5555
Participant passcode: 11111111#

Looking forward to meeting with you! Should you have any questions or need additional information, please feel free to contact me.

Best regards,
Steve Anyrep
steve.anyrep@anycompany.com
1-800-123-4567

## *Require Attendees to Follow the Three-Ten Rule*

The single biggest disruption to a remote demo (besides the Internet connection quitting, that is!) is trying to help attendees who are having difficulty logging into the Web conference. This usually occurs because one or more participants have never used the technology before, and they try logging in and doing the necessary downloads at the last minute. So if the meeting is supposed to begin at 1:00 p.m., you might have to spend the first 10 minutes or more walking people through the login steps over the phone. Other attendees are meanwhile getting impatient—and you end up rushing through the material once the real meeting finally begins.

You can use the *Three-Ten* rule to help minimize user problems from occurring during your demo:

**3** Require that attendees register and download any necessary software applet ***three*** days before the demo.

**10** Require that attendees log in ***ten*** minutes before the demo begins.

***Note!*** ***You will have limited success with getting people to log in before the top of the hour and staying past the bottom of the hour. So you should plan your demo to last 50 minutes or less. That way, attendees can log in at 1:00 p.m., for example, putting the presentation start time at 1:10, with a 2:00 hard stop.***

## *Establish Meeting Ground Rules*

Take a few moments before the meeting begins to ask that participants follow simple etiquette for the Web-based meeting, namely, the following: shut down all applications (especially e-mail!) besides the Web conference tool; and mute the phone to minimize background noise.

## *Use More Mouse and Less Keyboard*

In a face-to-face demo, using keyboard shortcuts can make your software look faster and more impressive. But in a remote situation, avoid shortcuts and use that mouse. Why? Because using the mouse requires more steps to accomplish tasks in the interface, you will be providing additional description as your pointer opens and closes various menus and dialog boxes on screen. In short, you will speak more and your desktop will look more active. It can be a challenge to hold someone's attention when he's alone in his office staring at a computer screen, so the more visual and auditory stimulus there is, the better.

## *Ask More Questions*

Have you ever attended a Web-based conference, and found better things to do while the host droned on? Like check your e-mail, grab a cup of coffee, or file your tax return? Most of us would answer in the affirmative, unfortunately. So how can you keep your audience engaged? Asking frequent questions is a great strategy.

Don't show more than three features without asking your audience if they understand. Ask "Does that make sense?" followed by "Who has a question on what I just covered?" That pair of questions will prompt most people to say "yes," and it gives other people an opening to ask questions without feeling like they're interrupting.

Direct a question to specific attendees. If someone in the meeting brought up a capability in a previous conversation, ask that person to chime in after you cover that feature in the demo. For example:

**Presenter:** "Nancy, I think you mentioned once that you needed a way to reduce requests for human translators in China. How do you think our expanded online Chinese dictionary feature will help?"

## *Use a Telephone Headset*

Relying on your speaker phone during the teleconference can be a risky proposition when you consider audio quality and background noise. And the last thing you want to do is cradle a phone between your ear and shoulder for an hour while you operate the computer and take notes. Invest in a good telephone headset instead. You'll maintain high-quality audio while keeping your hands free.

## *Build and Deliver an Offline Version of Your Demo*

As you prepare your demo, take screen captures of the salient points you will cover, and insert them into a PowerPoint slideshow. E-mail this slideshow to each participant the day before the Web conference. You've just created an effective backup demo that you can use if your Internet connection goes down. Simply have the attendees open the presentation and walk them through the slides over the phone. Is it as effective as a live demo? No. But has your preparedness made a favorable impression on your audience? Absolutely.

# Part Summary

In this part, you learned how to:

- ▶ Identify the characteristics of Web conferencing application software.
- ▶ Recognize the problems that cause online demos to occasionally fail.
- ▶ Maximize the effectiveness of your remote demos by mastering the conferencing application, limiting attendance, simplifying instructions, and establishing meeting ground rules.

# Viva-Crisp 50-Minute
# Titles in the Series

| ISBN | Author | Title | YOP | Price |
|---|---|---|---|---|
| 9788130918174 | Gambino | **50 Minutes to Better Software Demos**: *Apply Your Sales Skills with Confidence* | 2011 | 195.00 |
| 9788130918488 | Bozek | **50 One-Minute Tips to Better Communications**: *Speak, Write and Present More Effectively, 3/e* | 2011 | 250.00 |
| 9788130918211 | Conlow & Watsabaugh | **Achieving Supervisory Excellence**: *Be the Leader Your People Need* | 2011 | 195.00 |
| 9788130918396 | McKnight & Chapman | **Attitude**: *Protect Your Most Priceless Asset, 5/e* | 2011 | 245.00 |
| 9788130918495 | Terry Dickey | **Basics of Budgeting**: *Become a Better Business Planner, 2/e* | 2011 | 250.00 |
| 9788130918310 | Conlow & Watsabaugh | **Become a Successful Supervisor**: *Develop Essential People Skills* | 2011 | 225.00 |
| 9788130918327 | Brock | **Better Business Writing**: *Become A More Powerful Communicator, 5/e* | 2011 | 225.00 |
| 9788130918228 | Dupont | **Business Etiquette & Professionalism**: *Conduct Yourself With Confidence, 3/e* | 2011 | 195.00 |
| 9788130918181 | Morgan | **Calming Upset Customers**: *Stay in Control ... In any Situation, 4/e* | 2011 | 195.00 |
| 9788130918198 | Minor | **Coaching and Counseling**: *Become a Better Manager Through Mentoring, 4/e* | 2011 | 195.00 |
| 9788130918273 | Decker | **Communication Skills for Leaders**: *Deliver a Clear and Consistent Message, 4/e* | 2011 | 225.00 |
| 9788130918143 | Kindler | **Conflict Management**: *Resolve Disagreement at Work, 4/e* | 2011 | 165.00 |
| 9788130918280 | Conlow & Watsabaugh | **Creating a High Performance Team**: *Gain the Skills of Today's Successful Leaders* | 2011 | 225.00 |
| 9788130918334 | Feldman | **Critical Thinking**: *Make Strategic Decisions With Confidence, 2/e* | 2011 | 225.00 |
| 9788130918426 | Flynn | **E-Mail Management**: *Keep Your Inbox Under Control, 2/e* | 2011 | 245.00 |
| 9788130918471 | Kravitz & Schubert | **Emotional Intelligence Works**: *Think, Be and Work Smarter, 3/e* | 2011 | 245.00 |
| 9788130918150 | Maddux | **Ethics in Business**: *Manage With Authority and Fairness, 2/e* | 2011 | 195.00 |
| 9788130918235 | Rouillard | **Goals and Goal Setting**: *Achieve Measurable Results, 4/e* | 2011 | 195.00 |
| 9788130918204 | Conlow Watsabaugh | **Handling Difficult People and Situations**: *Lead People Through Adversity* | 2011 | 195.00 |

| ISBN | Author | Title | YOP | Price |
|---|---|---|---|---|
| 9788130918433 | Wendover | **High Performance Hiring**: *Select the Best Every Time, 3/e* | 2011 | 245.00 |
| 9788130918402 | Shea | **Making the Most of Being Mentored**: *Mentors Help Mentees Do, 2/e* | 2011 | 245.00 |
| 9788130918242 | Scott | **Managing Personal Change**: *Stay Positive and Stay in Control*, 3/e | 2011 | 195.00 |
| 9788130918341 | Haynes | **Meeting Skills for Leaders**: *Make Meetings More Productive, 4/e* | 2011 | 225.00 |
| 9788130918440 | Shea | **Mentoring**: *Make It A Mutually Rewarding Experience, 4/e* | 2011 | 245.00 |
| 9788130918525 | Shandler | **Motivating the Millennial Knowledge Worker**: *Help Today's Workforce Succeed in Today's Economy* | 2011 | 395.00 |
| 9788130918167 | Mandel | **Presentation Skills**: *Captivate and Educate Your Audience, 4/e* | 2011 | 195.00 |
| 9788130918518 | Pokras | **Problem Solving for Teams**: *Make Consensus More Achievable, 3/e* | 2011 | 295.00 |
| 9788130918259 | Haynes | **Project Management**: *Get from the Idea to Implementation Successfully, 4/e* | 2011 | 195.00 |
| 9788130918372 | Martin | **Quality Customer Service**: *Satisfy Customers– It's Everybody's Job, 5/e* | 2011 | 245.00 |
| 9788130918457 | Lightle & Doucet | **Sexual Harassment in the Workplace**: *Create a Better Workplace For Everyone, 3/e* | 2011 | 245.00 |
| 9788130918501 | Lengefeld | **Study Skills Strategies**: *Get the Most From Every Minute of Learning, 4/e* | 2011 | 250.00 |
| 9788130918358 | Conlow & Watsabaugh | **SuperSTAR Customer Service**: *It's all about C.A.R.E.* | 2011 | 225.00 |
| 9788130918297 | Maddux & Wingfield | **Team Building**: *Turn Personal Strengths Into Group Success, 5/e* | 2011 | 225.00 |
| 9788130918464 | Finch | **Telephone Courtesy & Customer Service**: *Be Your Company's Lifeline to Customers, 4/e* | 2011 | 245.00 |
| 9788130918389 | Conlow & Watsabaugh | **Telephone Skills that Satisfy Customers**: *Unleash the Full Potential of the Telephone* | 2011 | 245.00 |
| 9788130918303 | Romero | **The Business of Listening**: *Become a More Effective Listener, 4/e* | 2011 | 225.00 |
| 9788130918365 | Chapman & McKnight | **The New Supervisor**: *Lead With Confidence, 5/e* | 2011 | 225.00 |
| 9788130918266 | Haynes | **Time Management**: *Get An Extra Day a Week* | 2011 | 195.00 |
| 9788130918419 | Gill & Chatton | **Understanding Financial Statements**: *Master the Tools That Help You Succeed, 3/e* | 2011 | 245.00 |